THERE WERE ZULUS AT THE BOTTOM OF OUR GARDEN

GW00707617

Margaret Heard

ARTHUR H. STOCKWELL LTD.
Elms Court   Ilfracombe
Devon

ISBN 0 7223 1910-X
Printed in Great Britain by
Arthur H. Stockwell Ltd.
Elms Court   Ilfracombe
Devon

CONTENTS

This book is dedicated to my husband John A. who is my severest critic. Also Mr John Hughes without whose help and guidance it would never have been written; my son Richard who gave me encouragement, and my friend Renee Drew, who has asked me many times during the last fifty years to write my childhood story. Finally, to my other children: Elizabeth, Mary, Michael, Lorina, Georgina and Kathleen, who have given me many happy years.

Preface

Although this story is primarily of my birth and childhood in Natal, South Africa, I have endeavoured to present a brief history of the Zulu nation, as it was for almost a hundred years, 1783-1879.

The most exciting part of the history I learnt from Sixpence, our aged houseboy, who had been a Zulu warrior chieftain. He was a wonderful raconteur, vividly bringing to life the world he had lived in, and how he had battled and suffered in his youth.

On every page of the history books I had to study at school, a veritable cascade of facts and dates emerged. At that time I wasn't very interested, but over the years the Zulu lifestyle really captured my imagination, as I began to realise what an intensely pulsating, tragic, happy and energetic life the Zulu nation had lived.

I don't pretend to be a writer, but my children are anxious that I should put on record some of the events which have made my life an interesting one. Stories get so changed in the telling, especially if there is anything unusual or uncommon in them, that my children think I should narrate some of my childhood experiences just as they happened.

So, without further ado, I will begin.

Chapter 1

The start of the Zulu nation under Chaka's rule

South Africa, land of my birth and childhood — but before writing my own story I would like to tell you a little about the ancestors of the Zulus, who lived in their kraal at the bottom of our garden, and how, from a pastoral people they were forged into one of the strongest warrior nations under a despotic and tyrannical king called Chaka (1783-1828). They became the most powerful people in South Africa and the most feared.

Before Chaka's rise to power, Zululand and Natal were free and peaceful territories in which a mixture of independent tribes lived. The general name for these people was Nguni and they inhabited both the east coast lands of South Africa and the central section of Rhodesia. The tribes were variously called Zulu, Xhosa, Swazi and Ndebele. They all spoke a related language, lived similar lives and were ruled by their own tribal chiefs.

The Zulus loved the land, tilling the soil and planting crops which were tended with great care. They were expert hunters, snaring and trapping animals and whilst hunting, they would collect all edible roots, berries and bulbs, thereby keeping their food store filled. They were also great cattlemen as the more cattle a chief had, the more he was respected.

The men of the kraal, after their day's work was done, used to enjoy a life of comparative ease. Smoking, drinking their home-brewed beer, swapping stories and memories under a shady tree. This tranquil life ceased as soon as Chaka, a noted Zulu chief, took possession of the Zulu throne in 1816. He intended to form a strong and disciplined military army. He was therefore determined to train those Zulus who lived north

7

of the Tugela River in Natal, approximately 50 miles from Pietermaritzburg, to be warriors. The men of the Zulu kraals had always been admired for the magnificence of their physique, and when they became a nation, this admiration was extended to their fighting qualities.

After a series of victorious campaigns under Chaka, they became masters of the country from the Zambezi River to the Cape of Good Hope, and their influence was felt as far north as Lake Victoria.

Chaka, because of his cruelty and tyranny, was eventually murdered by his half-brother Dingaan (more of him later). Whilst Chaka ruled, South African territories were fortified with military kraals manned with powerful army regiments. These kraals were always strategically placed on river banks, hilltops, or mountain slopes. Apart from defending Chaka's empire, they were the headquarters from which the warriors were sent on destructive raids into neighbouring territories.

Military kraals were always built to the same plan, grass huts being erected side by side to form a circle, approximately one mile in circumference. Huge thick branches of a very prickly thorn-bush were built round the camp to make a hedge. The large arena in the centre was used for the assembly of the regiments on important occasions and it was also used as a cattle-fold for the royal herd.

When the warriors were dressed in their full regalia and chanting their war songs, they were a truly awe-inspiring sight, especially when dancing to their singing and to the throb, throb, throbbing of the tom-toms. They whirled and twirled, leaping into the air and twisting their bodies and at the same time stamping and shuffling their feet, carrying long stabbing spears and a couple of assegais — slender spears of hard wood tipped with iron. The dance I witnessed was many years afterwards. An attraction put on for the benefit of visitors, which was danced to the following war song:

> We journey to war, over the hills and yonder,
> over the hills where the sun sets, to a
> country we do not know.
> We journey for you King and Father, lion;
> elephant; liberator; King of Kings; King
> of the Zulu Dingaan.

The noise of the chanting, drumming, and the thudding and shuffling of the warriors' feet will remain with me all my life. After the war dance we watched the ceremonial dance, which was accompanied by a very harmonious type of singing and was a joy to see. The final part, which was the Royal Salute, was the best and was made by striking the assegais on the shields. It began with a low murmuring, like the sound of the sea, which grew louder and louder until it exploded into a crescendo, like far off thunder, and finished with a sharp, quick rattle.

The royal women's quarters, which housed the king's hand-picked concubines, were a very important part of a military kraal. They were always sited at the top end of the camp, and were supervised by an older woman appointed by the king. Chaka had chosen Mkabayi, one of his aunts, to be head of the whole settlement, and to supervise his royal camp at a place called emBelebeni (place of endless worry) which guarded the approaches to emAkhosini (the place of kings), a burial ground of notable ancestors of the tribe and the most sacred spot in all Zululand. It was situated on a tree-covered ridge some ten miles from the meeting place of two waters: Umkumbane — a stream, and the white Umfalozi River. There were several regiments of very experienced warriors stationed in this camp, forming a division of the Zulu army.

As his first move in the creation of a strong Zulu nation, Chaka usurped the chief in 1816, upsetting the whole of the Nguni clan. He was a very arrogant young man, determined to achieve power and control a nation of warriors. He immediately set about conscripting all the young men for military training and then decreed that only men between twenty and thirty who excelled in battle would be allowed to marry! He didn't like married men at all, considering them to be soft; but that didn't stop him from forming them into a regiment as well.

He conceived a very practical system of warfare, by forming units of Zulu warriors and making them so proficient in combat that they could be called upon at any given moment (similar to the territorial units of today). Because of their training in hand-to-hand combat with small throwing assegai, instead of using the old-fashioned long-bladed spear, they became a force to be reckoned with. Apart from that, he threatened them with death if they dared to return home from a battle without their weapons and not being victorious, as he considered this to be cowardice in the face of the enemy.

Battle formations looked exactly like the head of a two-horned beast; the horns would extend for miles away behind the hills, then gradually they would draw together until suddenly the enemy would find themselves completely surrounded, as did the British at Isandhlwana and other battlefields, before the Zulu was defeated and conquered. The Russians used precisely the same tactics in the Second World War, to devastating effect.

Chaka brooked no interference and if anyone spoke ill of him he would have them disembowelled and roasted over a hot fire. He had all neighbouring villages raided, pillaging and massacring all the people except young men, who were immediately drafted into his army.

This 'iron leader' made conquest after conquest until he eventually extended his territories, and was acknowledged as supreme ruler over all the people living in the regions bounded by the Tugela River in the south, the Pongolo in the north, the Nyati River in the west and the Indian Ocean in the east, calling the whole of the conquered area Zululand. By this time his army had grown to gigantic proportions and was very much feared. Especially as he exterminated all who stood in his way and razed the opposing kraals to the ground.

Knowing he needed time to organise and administer his new vast kingdom, Chaka now took a break from warfare. During this peaceful period, he moved to a new royal kraal, supervising its construction. It was three times as large as the old one, being three miles in circumference and standing on a hill overlooking the western limits of Umhlatuze Valley. It has been said that there were 1300-1400 huts for warriors and 100 for his concubines. When he considered his new kraal impregnable, his first act of 'civil administration' was to send for all the tribal chiefs and clansmen who he thought might be disloyal and have them all executed. Even his own immediate relatives were terrified in case they put a foot wrong and would be killed as well. Soon this new kraal of his became the most feared and hated place in all Zululand.

Trials were an absolute farce, as he presided over them all at the tribal court in Bulawayo; he was also such an impatient man that he would never listen to lengthy speeches. To cut them short he usually passed the death sentence by bellowing *'msuseni'* (take him away), or he would lift his finger, or nod his head, which meant the prisoner would be taken away and killed on the outskirts of Bulawayo.

His people were now so frightened of him that many perished by throwing themselves over a precipice, sooner than face being put to death by disembowellment with the Zulu stabbing-spear.

Resentment was now growing apace. Warriors and their families were really upset at the military war-machine which had changed so much of their lives, and thought longingly of their previous free and peaceful existence. They were particularly disturbed with Chaka's new decree relating to the 'Festival of the First Fruits' (Umkhosi), a ceremony held in December, when the crops were ripening and the full moon was due. Each kraal would get things ready for feasting and dancing as soon as the moon appeared, when the chief and all his subjects would sing sacred songs and dance for three days and nights.

It was the most religious festival of the year, as they were praising their ancestral spirits and pleading with the Great Great One to protect their crops from pestilence, drought, hail, insects and torrential rains. On the final day the climax would be a fight between a fierce black bull and a group of unarmed warriors. When the bull collapsed under a hail of clenched fists, after a prolonged fight, it would be stabbed to death by the chief's witch-doctor. A great feast followed when the first fruits of the ripening crops would be eaten.

The decree that caused such apprehension, stated that no kraal would be allowed to hold its own festival but all would have to travel to Bulawayo where Chaka wanted it held. This meant that everyone in Zululand had to report to the capital well in advance of the full moon, and death would be the punishment for failure to attend. This was the final straw for two dignitaries — Dingaan (the Needy One) and Mhlangana (the Little Reed) — who detested Chaka, their half-brother, as did the aunt called Mkabayi, who Chaka had appointed as supervisor of his royal seraglio. She was utterly convinced that only Chaka's death would bring peace to the country again. (Chapters 2 and 3 deal with these people and their scheme to get rid of the King.)

The reason the individual clans were worried was that by going to Bulawayo the Great Great One would be upset and not look after their crops. They also felt that he would be so angry, he would eventually destroy the Zulu nation; but their main worry was that they would not be back in time to reap their, hopefully, abundant harvest to store in their granaries.

In 1824 two ships arrived off the coast of Natal. They anchored in Port Natal, where traders and hunters, consisting of Englishmen, Dutch, Germans, French, Hottentots and a Dane, disembarked. Food, firearms, ammunition, horses and 'goods' for bartering were also unloaded.

Chaka learned of them quite by accident, as a few weeks before they arrived a man called Jacob (a member of the Xhosa tribe, who had been employed by the white traders as an interpreter), had been picked up by a Zulu scouting party and taken straight to the royal kraal, where he was asked what he was doing in Zulu territory. He explained he had been acting as an interpreter to the 'floating houses' which were sailing near the coast. Chaka was very interested in these 'floating houses', wanted to know everything about them, and eagerly awaited their arrival.

He eventually met the traders, a Lieutenant Farewell and Mr Fynn, who were paving the way for other traders, hunters, explorers, scientists, missionaries and anyone else who wanted to pursue interests in Zulu territory — also for the Boer commanders and British regiments, who were eventually to destroy the power of the Zulu and colonize the area.

The king took a great liking to these traders, with their stories of other lands, but what interested him most was the different kinds of 'goods' they had brought with them for bartering, such as cheap jewellery that glittered and sparkled, brightly coloured materials, mirrors, combs and an assortment of beads which were highly prized by the Zulu women. He kept Jacob on as his own interpreter to help with any bartering problems he may have, and gave him the nickname of 'swimmer' after hearing he had saved the master of one of the ships from drowning.

Traders began to settle in Port Natal, building homes and stockades in which to keep their horses. Chaka envied them their horses and guns and decided he must have these things for himself. He sent his warriors into Natal, but found his prey had vanished. The traders had received news of his intentions and fled to the south. Chaka's men chased the Zulus who had taken refuge from his tyranny in Natal, managing to catch the women, children, and not so fleet of foot, butchering them all.

Dingaan's hatred was now at boiling point. He knew he couldn't let Chaka's murders and despotism go on for much longer, but also knew he would have to wait for the right moment. He began to formulate various plans for Chaka's assassination. In discussing the matter with his brother, Mhlangana, they decided it would be a good idea to visit their Aunt Mkabayi and talk the matter over with her. Thus the seeds of a plot to get rid of a hated tyrant began to germinate.

Chapter 2

Mkabayi — Dingaan — Mhlangana — plotting Chaka's assassination

Mkabayi was born a twin in 1760 and, by rights, either she or her twin Mmama should have been slain, as it was considered an ominous event; but her father, an ancestral chief of the Zulu clan called Jama, refused to listen to his councillors and witch-doctors, who pleaded with him not to delay but to kill one of them at once. It was an incredible thing to do, as twins were supposed to be a threat to his life and he would always be in danger. The elders of the clan were astounded by his forbearance, but in an effort to solicit protection for him from the spirit world, they immediately slaughtered a cow for a sacrifice.

As they grew older the twins were cold-shouldered by all who knew the circumstances of their birth, all that is except their immediate family. Mkabayi grew sullen, moody and quick-tempered. The only person she could talk to was her father. She hated all men and her hatred intensified as she grew older, so although she was reputed to be physically attractive she remained a spinster all her life.

No one could believe that Jama would be spared to live into comparative old age and die from natural causes, which he did, but sixty years later the curse on the Zulu royal house was fulfilled with the assassination of Chaka, conceived and instigated by the elder twin, Mkabayi. When her father Jama died in 1781, because her younger brother Senzangakhona (heir apparent) had not been circumcised,* she and one of Jama's nephews became temporarily in control, whilst her

---

*After undergoing the tribal ritual of circumcision, a youth was then considered to have obtained his manhood.

14

sister Mmama was content to remain quietly in the bosom of her family.

Mkabayi refused to be dominated by the councillors and executed all whom she suspected of being disloyal to the Zulu kingdom. She stuck scrupulously to the traditions that had been passed on by her ancestors for generations. Although apparently accepting the break in tradition which had spared the life of herself and her twin.

Because of her temper she acquired the nickname of 'wild cat' and she was far from popular, but when her brother Senzangakhona ascended the throne a few years later (he reigned for thirty years) and she had to retire to another kraal, the dignitaries, almost to a man, confessed to a sneaking admiration for the fiery, quarrelsome but capable daughter of Jama.

Dingaan had always been Mkabayi's favourite. She considered that he and not Chaka should have been the royal chief, as he was the legitimate son of Senzangakhona and his sixth wife Mpikase, whilst Chaka was the illegitimate son of his mistress Nandi (the sweet one).

No one knows very much about Dingaan's life apart from the fact that he had been born and brought up in a royal kraal and was a very healthy boy, the sturdiest of his age group. At puberty, about twelve years of age, he was very broad-shouldered with heavy thighs, and by fourteen had grown as tall as the adults who attended his father. He was quick to anger when teased, but was too lazy to get into fights. One thing about him, though, was his obsession with cleanliness. He couldn't bear dirt or being unclean, so spent most of the day bathing in the streams and smoothing his skin with animal fat until it shone.

Dingaan (the needy one) was unable to make any close childhood friends except his sister Bayeka and his supposedly half-wit brother Mpanda (the root). When in later years Dingaan became a figure to be reckoned with, only three people understood his complex character, his sister and two senior officers (indunas) in the army.

He was thought to be about twenty-two years old in 1816, when his father died whilst he was away. He returned at once and on reaching the border, was just in time to learn that his clan was in mourning for a second time, as Chaka had returned to usurp the Zulu throne and had assassinated the newly elected chief.

Dingaan had never been ambitious as it was contrary to his spiritless disposition, but he now thought how ridiculous it was for this illegitimate son to sit on the throne as he, Dingaan, was far more eligible.

Whilst Chaka was subjugating Zululand, it is not known what part Dingaan was taking, as neither in the early writings of white men, nor in the legends of the present day Zulu is important reference made to his early years in Chaka's army, but one thing is certain, he was never reported for cowardice as he would have been executed.

During July 1828, Chaka prepared for another campaign, sending all of his regiments except two on this new expedition. Of the regiments remaining, one consisted only of adolescent boys, and the other was made up of retired warriors, cattlemen and menial workers. The army left at the end of the month and was the largest ever to cross the borders of Zululand. Chaka himself during this time was living in a royal kraal, built in 1825 between two rivers, the Nonoti and the Umvati, spending most of his time with his royal concubines. During the next few weeks he executed about four hundred wives of the warriors who were away with the army, as he thought they were all practising witchcraft.

Meanwhile the army, with their indunas (warriors of rank) in command, was pushing its way through the bushveld (grass country made up largely of woodland) of Northern Zululand, reaching territory governed by a chief who was the father of Mbosha, Chaka's servant, and there they stayed for a few days. Dingaan and Mhlangana claimed they felt ill and incapable of going further with the army into Portuguese East Africa. As soon as they were thought capable of the journey, they were sent home, much to their delight.

Whilst the army was away, Mkabayi, overseer of the seraglio, had made it a hot-bed of intrigue by whispering words of rebellion into the ears of dignitaries whom she knew feared and hated Chaka. She was also well aware of the secret meetings by conspirators that had been taking place, and so was able to fan the flames of revolt. As a further contribution to the unrest, she began spreading rumours that Chaka had actually killed his mother; she had *not* died from an illness, as originally thought. How long would the people tolerate Chaka, who put to death not only his enemies but also his own mother?

Word reached Dingaan telling him to return, as the time had come to act — hence his pretended illness. He and his brother Mhlangana journeyed first to Bulawayo. Finding that Chaka was in fact at a place called Dukuza, they made their way there, and sent a young herdsboy to find Chaka's servant Mbaspha, who they knew hated Chaka too, telling the lad to secretly inform Mbaspha that Dingaan and Mhlangana had returned and wished to speak with him. Mbaspha arrived soon afterwards and the three set about planning the death of Chaka.

On the 22nd September 1828 Dingaan and Mhlangana hid small stabbing-spears under their cloaks and walked to the kraal. On entering, they found Chaka sitting on a stool, wrapped in a kaross (South African skin blanket) admiring his herds in the cattle-fold. They moved very slowly towards him but suddenly messengers from the south, a group of warriors, walked into the kraal bearing gifts for the king.

Dingaan and his two co-conspirators darted behind a hedge to wait for a better opportunity. It wasn't until the sun was setting that Mbaspha made a move. An assegai in one hand and a knobkerrie in the other, he slunk along the hedge to an opening, then suddenly dashed into the open and bore down on the warriors, whom he proceeded to beat unmercifully for allegedly thrusting themselves on the king's privacy. Chaka was astounded and stood up to remonstrate with Mbaspha but suddenly screamed in agony as stabbing-spears, thrust by Dingaan and Mhlangana, plunged deep into his back. Turning slowly Chaka looked at his brothers and met their murderous gaze. He staggered and reeled to the kraal gate, leaving a blood trail and dropping his blood-soaked kaross on the floor of the cattle-fold. As he fell he implored them to spare his life but Mbaspha plunged an assegai straight into the king's body. Chaka's dying words to Dingaan were, "You'll not rule long. This country will soon be overrun by the white man."

Chapter 3

The acceptance of Dingaan as king

Discussing what to do with the body, at first they thought of throwing it in the river and letting the crocodiles do their worst, but Dingaan said it should have a proper burial as befitting a Zulu king. As it was getting dark they decided to leave the body where it was till morning, as they were too frightened to stay there in case Chaka's spirit might appear. They left quickly and went to a hiding place which Mbaspha had previously found for them.

When they went back next day the body was still there and hadn't been eaten by any animal during the night. Dingaan immediately sent a group of youths to tell the people they must come and attend Chaka's burial. An ox had been chosen from the royal herd to be slaughtered as a sacrifice. Chaka's body was wrapped in hide which was bound with cords, made from a rope creeper, then his belongings were brought out and placed by the body.

One of Chaka's loyal councillors condemned Dingaan and Mhlangana for murdering him and asked the people to have them killed, but Dingaan made a speech and asked them if they hadn't had enough of Chaka's tyranny and weren't they glad to be delivered from all their miseries? They could now start to sing, dance and be merry once again.

The Zulu clans didn't even listen to the councillor but rejoined, and with one voice claimed Dingaan and Mhlangana as their deliverers, giving thanks to the Great Great One for their deliverance from Chaka, the despot and tyrant.

Arrangements then went on for the funeral to take place. The body with its belongings was lowered into the chosen,

18

dried up, old grain-pit which was in the cattle-fold. When filled, it was covered with stones and mimosa thorn-bush branches were piled on top. The adjacent grain-pit had pieces of oxen meat placed in it, to appease the ghost of Chaka should it be hungry. The other grain-pits were very tightly covered to prevent Chaka's spirit coming out and punishing the assassins.

Dingaan, Mhlangana and Myboshi then washed their hands and rinsed their mouths with a vile concoction of ox blood and gall (greenish-yellow secretion taken from the ox liver), which was supposed to purify them, thereby cleansing them of the sin of murder.

When the funeral was over the people moved into the cattle-fold to sing, feast, dance and generally make merry. The only people to be upset were the concubines, who were weeping and wailing and seemed genuinely unhappy.

It was decided and agreed by Dingaan and Mhlangana, that they would go to another kraal to await the arrival of the army for them to nominate the new king, but first of all Dingaan journeyed to tell his Aunt Mkabayi that her plan for the assassination of Chaka had been successful.

Weeks went by and although the brothers lived in different huts, next door to each other, and spent hours drinking beer and talking about their accomplishments to date, they were getting very, very argumentative, vying with each other to prove their worthiness to be the next Zulu king.

Dingaan became very moody but Mhlangana took no notice, being used to these moody periods. This made Dingaan more angry than ever, even to the point of wanting to kill Mhlangana; but instead, he went to see his aunt again and told her all his troubles. She told him not to worry as she would see that Mhlangana died.

Soon afterwards someone tried to murder Dingaan himself! He was settling down to sleep one night, when a stabbing-spear was thrown. It only grazed him but made him really worried. He was convinced that it was his brother's doing.

Mkabayi sent some of her messengers to ask Mhlangana to go and see her. They were to tell him that she was worried because a new king hadn't as yet been nominated, and she did not think it necessary to wait any longer for the army to arrive, therefore she wanted to discuss the matter with him immediately. He felt very elated and went at once, thinking she must also believe he should be next in line. As she was such a powerful personage, he knew that with her nomination, the throne would be his with no trouble at all.

Arriving at the royal kraal, he went straight to see his aunt at the seraglio. The meeting began with an exchange of greetings, but then she stared at him with hypnotic eyes, which have been described as 'two circles of fire', and told him she was very disturbed indeed to hear of the quarrels between him and Dingaan. She went on to accuse him of instigating these quarrels so that he could eventually have an excuse to kill Dingaan, thereby ensuring that he, Mhlangana, would be the next king even though he had agreed to wait for the arrival of the army. Mhlangana emphatically denied these accusations, protesting that it was the other way round and that Dingaan was the one seeking the throne.

Mkabayi then sent for Dingaan, who had arrived earlier by arrangement. She asked for his version (which, of course, she already knew) then said she would meet them next morning by the riverside at a given spot, to let them know who she would nominate.

Next morning only one turned up to keep the appointment — Mhlangana. He was seized and taken away by four of Dingaan's men. Later in the day his death was announced by his aunt in the royal kraal.

Mkabayi had a long talk with Dingaan and told him he must go to Dukuza and tell the people who were living in the royal kraal that he would take over the throne until the army arrived, then to send messengers to the other kraals to let them know his decision.

Meanwhile the army was having troubles of its own. It had been reduced by battles and dysentery, with hundreds of warriors dying, and although they were only ten days march from Dukuza, they were afraid to return home without being victorious, as it would mean death; but one of the officers said he would prefer to die in his own land as a warrior, than be exiled in a foreign territory.

On nearing Dukuza they heard of Chaka's death and there was a great roar of approval. They openly rejoiced at

Dingaan's courage and arriving at the royal kraal, they greeted him with the title 'your Royal Highness'. All except one officer called Mdlaka. He said Dingaan didn't deserve to be acclaimed king and should be executed for murder but no one listened and he, with his few followers, hurriedly left the royal kraal. It was thus that Dingaan became king of Zululand.

Chapter 4

Dingaan the king

As soon as Dingaan was proclaimed king a great feast was held, using cattle slaughtered from the royal herd. Great quantities of home-brewed beer were quaffed and a wonderful time was had by all, with much singing, dancing and eating.

Dingaan was an extremely complex person, proving later to be one of the most interesting antagonists of the Boers. Moving from the kraal in Dukuza, he went with his royal concubines, his complete clan and all the servants to the ancestral royal kraal Nobamba, which was situated at emAkhosina (the place of the kings).

At first Dingaan believed that diplomacy was a better way to achieve his ends than fighting. He used to play one opponent off against another, thereby keeping a very delicate state of tension amongst his officers. When he did strike, he did so swiftly and without warning.

Eventually becoming besotted with his own power, he made visitors crawl toward him on their hands and knees, whilst he reclined at ease among his wives, reputed to number almost a hundred. Mostly though, he sat on a throne which had been made for him by his loyal officers. When feeling angry, he would often interview strangers across a wall of stakes, whilst peering at them through a fringe of beads which he wore on his forehead.

Although finding white people fascinating and interesting, he was dubious about their interests in his country. At the same time he was anxious to make friends with the traders in Port Natal. Sometimes he would be very genial and friendly but suddenly he would turn vicious and would condemn someone to death for just being near him, or not near enough. He would usually meet people wearing a green baize coarse woollen blanket, which covered his heavy, stocky figure.

A few months after being declared king, Dingaan decided to build a new military camp, to be called emGungungdlovi (the place surrounded by elephants) near the 'Valley of the Zulu', which was the birthplace and resting place of the great chief called Zulu, founder of the original Zulu clan; and many other 'notables' of the tribe were buried there.

The 'Valley of the Zulu' was a very fertile piece of land with many streams, which kept the green grazing land very 'lush' indeed, as it was so well watered. Dingaan had his kraal built there as he intended to make it his capital and to use the kraal as a gigantic military camp. It eventually became the most hated and feared place in all South Africa.

The women were used to fetch and carry grass and reeds, which were needed for making and thatching the beehive huts. Work considered too hard for women was done by the warriors; for example, digging holes for the flexible poles which were so pliable they could be pulled into any shape required. Needless to say, Dingaan's hut was the most spacious of them all and the largest; lit only by daylight coming through the low door, it was very dark and sombre, although the floor looked as if it had been polished as it had been greased and rubbed so often. It was approximately twenty feet in diameter and height, so that it towered over the rest of the kraal. The kraal was built on a hilltop which enabled Dingaan to see the whole of the camp and also much of the surrounding countryside.

The main camp entrance was at the western end of the circle of huts. It looked like a long passage running from the outer to the inner hedges which surrounded the arena. The entrance was always under guard so that a stranger could not get near the king.

There were reputed to be about twenty to thirty thousand warriors living in the kraal, as well as warriors whom Dingaan was holding as hostages for the good behaviour of their families. He was now becoming very arrogant and if one of his subjects so much as sneezed in front of him he would have them executed.

About a year after becoming king in March 1829, some white traders came to visit him and although they had heard of his friendliness to whites, they pitched their tents just outside the royal kraal. Dingaan invited them in and immediately asked what gifts they had brought him. They were most embarrassed as no one had thought about it, but on the spur of the moment said they had heard how fond he was of cattle and knew how valuable they were to the king, so had a magnificent ox for him, which they hoped he would accept; actually it was one of the oxen which was pulling their wagon!

The traders enjoyed their stay at the royal kraal, being very well treated, with as much to eat and drink as they wished. Their notes later described Dingaan as a kind-hearted, considerate king. They also added that he was extremely popular and 'every inch' a king, with a natural dignity and sympathetic nature.

When the time came for them to leave, to join up with a group of other traders at Delagoa Bay, Dingaan gave them a symbolised note, to show to the various chiefs of the land which they would have to pass through on their way to the bay. This note requested all the chiefs to provide for them on the journey. The traders told Dingaan they would be back with many gifts in return for his hospitality. Unfortunately this did not happen as, within a few weeks, they died from 'swamp fever' in Portuguese East Africa.

A few months after his ascension to the throne, June 1829, Dingaan heard that Mdlaka, the officer who had refused to acknowledge him as king, and several other officers, were plotting rebellion. Dingaan had Mdlaka put to death, then, rounding up the others, he killed them, their wives, children and servants, and completely 'gutted' their kraals by fire. The Zulu clans suddenly realised they had rid themselves of one despot only to be saddled with another, and that tyranny was once more the order of the day. Hundreds now fled to Natal to join the Black Colony which was already there, made up of refugees who had previously fled Chaka's rule.

Dingaan's place of execution was near the royal kraal and was called kwaMatwane, after the particularly ghastly killing of Chief Matwane, who had been one of those who fled Chaka's rule. When Dingaan took over, Matwane returned and asked to serve him. This Dingaan granted and Matwane was sent to live in 'The Valley of the Kings'.

Soon afterwards, Dingaan went to live in emGungungdlovi. He sent an invitation to Matwane and his followers to visit him in the great arena, but when they arrived he promptly told his executioners to take them away. They gouged out Matwane's eyes and thrust pointed sticks up his nostrils before breaking his neck. His followers were beaten to death with knobkerries (truncheons) by the guards. Following this incident many more Zulus (and white people) were murdered there, on the express order of Dingaan.

When Dingaan first became king he wanted to please the people, so he relaxed many of Chaka's harsh rules, including the strict discipline from which the regiments had suffered. They were now allowed to marry when they wished and warriors were even permitted to leave the army. All military expeditions into alien territory were also suspended.

Unfortunately this led to many of the Zulu clans wanting to go back to being tribal, with their own chiefs, breaking away from the large Zulu clan. Dingaan didn't like this one bit, re-imposing strict discipline; to keep the army strong and just to keep them busy, he sent them off to pillage their neighbours' territories once again.

Dingaan determined to seek the friendship of the white traders. He already knew and liked many of the English who lived in Natal, and was exceptionally fond of listening to the stories which were told by the missionaries about their 'God'. He thought the whites must be very clever people and encouraged them to visit him, offering ivory and antelope hides in exchange for gifts.

In the meantime Jacob (his interpreter) was poisoning Dingaan's mind against white men, who he said were cruel and treacherous. He, Jacob, had also heard that the British were preparing to overthrow Dingaan. Believing all this to be true, Dingaan began to distrust the traders in Port Natal and only tolerated them because of the many gifts they brought him. He was very acquisitive and loved receiving novelties of all kinds. He would immediately try them out; and one of the stories told is about his interest in magnifying glasses. One day he held such a glass over the arm of one of his servants, just to see the sun's rays burn a hole through the skin!

The traders weren't very happy with his friendliness as they never knew when he would ask for more gifts, especially as he did not keep his word over the ivory and antelope skins; but if they had the temerity to question him, he would immediately accuse them of harbouring runaway slaves whom he wished to slay.

Amongst the traders was a Jew called Isaac. Dingaan greatly admired this man and was particularly interested in his musket. One day Isaac was invited to go and see Dingaan, and was asked to take his gun with him. When he arrived he saw Dingaan surrounded by his councillors, talking to two women who turned out to be widows of renegade chiefs who had killed the trader Lieutenant Farewell. Dingaan was so incensed at this particular murder that he had sent his warriors after the culprits to cudgel them to death. Not content with that, he had decided the women should die as well and as Farewell had been British, thought it fitting that Isaac should shoot them to revenge his compatriot.

Isaac was shattered and pleaded for the women's lives, but Dingaan was emphatic that they should die. Isaac then told him that if he (Isaac) did the killing, he would be arrested and charged with murder on arrival back in Natal. Dingaan was furious and refused to listen. He ordered one of Isaac's Zulu servants to take the gun and shoot the women. At first Isaac refused to hand over his gun, but aware of the danger to the whole of his party, had no option but to comply.

When he was describing the scene later, Isaac said his servant Nasapongo went to within ten yards of the women and fired. The bullet went straight through the first woman's breast, killing her instantly. The warriors who were guarding the women panicked and ran away. The other woman didn't understand at all what had happened and stood still, holding a mat in front of her face, although she didn't know for what! Suddenly she saw Nasapongo coming toward her and started to run. He fired and hit her in the back, but only wounded her. He then reloaded, fired once more and killed her.

Dingaan was so impressed with the power of firearms that he praised and honoured Isaac as his most highly esteemed friend. This really worried Isaac, who had previously admired the king and thought there would be peace and prosperity throughout Zululand. He now realised that the rumours he had been hearing about executions of women and children, as well as warriors, were true, and after witnessing the cold-blooded murder of the two widows, realised there was another tyrant on the throne, and one who would prove to be even more formidable than Chaka, because Dingaan would combine diplomatic treachery with murderous intent.

Isaac's suspicions were heightened when several days later Dingaan sent for him again, and this time questioned him closely about the differences between the Zulu army and British soldiers. Isaac saw no harm in explaining the system of regiments, battalions, and platoons of the British army, and said that marksmanship with firearms was only achieved with strict discipline and training.

Dingaan next called his regiments together in the large arena and initiated a discussion amongst the officers, with regard to the power of the Zulu army and the white soldiers in South Africa. Most of the warriors considered they could wipe out the soldiers whilst they were reloading, as just after firing they were virtually helpless until the single-shot weapons were reloaded. Dingaan upbraided them, saying that when the guns went off they would all run away because they were afraid and that it was stupid to underestimate your enemy.

The crunch came for Isaac when Dingaan began questioning him about his rifle and pistol, asking to be shown in detail how they worked and for a demonstration firing at a tree. After the demonstration, Dingaan asked if he could have the gun to frighten away the witches when they roamed about his camp at night. Isaac refused, as he thought the less Dingaan knew about firearms the better, and the more respect he would have for the white man. Isaac also decided it was high time to get out and he therefore asked Dingaan's permission to leave. His request was granted and Dingaan gave him a gift of six milch cows and wished him a safe journey.

It was about this time that Dingaan began to encourage missionaries into his territory to instruct his people in Christianity. Sir Lowery Cole, the Cape governor, came to hear of it but didn't believe the reasons Dingaan gave. Writing to the Prime Minister, he asked permission to send an official to the port who could ascertain Dingaan's real interest. Unfortunately the British government didn't consider it an urgent matter, since up till then they had heard such glowing accounts of Dingaan (in fact it wasn't until 1843 that Henry Cloete was appointed Her Majesty's Commissioner for Natal).

Before the missionaries arrived it was rumoured that Dingaan meant to wage war against all the Zulu chiefs who were living in Natal, and he was under the impression that the white man would help him with guns and ammunition. The Zulu clans also thought this would happen, and although they had been told over and over again that it wouldn't many were too frightened to stay and started to move their cattle and people inland, begging the traders and white people to flee as well. Although the traders didn't really believe it, they sent out 'scouts' who learned that two regiments of the Zulu army were already on their way and were bent on massacring everyone in sight. Mr Fynn, one of the traders, immediately took refuge with his people in the bush and waited to see what would happen.

A scout had been stationed near Natal, and he reported that the deserted settlement had been looted and ransacked, and all the cattle had been taken to Dingaan. He also reported hearing that the regiments were trying to catch the refugees to kill them. Mr Fynn went further inland to reach a rocky stronghold, approximately twenty miles to the south of the port.

The Zulus eventually left to go back to the royal kraal, and Fynn and his people returned to the port; but for security's sake, a brig called the *St Michael* stayed in the mouth of the bay and fired her guns periodically each day. This was done so that any Zulu spy in the vicinity would report it to Dingaan, who they were sure wouldn't attack again whilst the ship remained where she was.

The king was supposedly very upset because the white man didn't trust him; he said that if they had stayed where they were he would not have hurt any white person. All he wanted to do was to execute his own people who should not have been there.

The first missionary to call on Dingaan was a man named Allen Gardener, and they met in June 1837. Dingaan had been watching his approach through a telescope from his kraal, and went to meet him. After talking together for several hours, Dingaan asked Gardener to build a mission station on a small hill which overlooked Dingaan's capital emGungungdlovi (the place surrounded by elephants), about a mile and a half to the north-east. Gardener actually went to arrange a full time missionary to be attached to the king's clan. Dingaan was absolutely delighted and said, as a mark of esteem, he would see Gardener at the ancestral royal kraal.

In due course, the Reverend Owen arrived by ox-wagon, feeling he was about to embark on one of the highlights of his career. Dingaan was delighted with him, as he had had the foresight to take a pictorial encyclopedia in his luggage, which so absorbed the king that he questioned Owen for hours, wanting to know every detail about every picture. His main interest was in peoples of foreign lands and the differences in their cultures, with especial interest in the difference between the English and the Boers. He always called the English 'George's children', and had previously thought the Boers were rebels of the English king and this was why they were running away from English territory.

Owen, relating his first meeting with Dingaan, described how the king was seated on his throne with a blanket covering him and looking very impressive. He took an immediate liking to this most renowned of Zulus, and was amazed at the speed with which his slightest wish was carried out.

The mission station had already been built on the orders of Dingaan and was waiting for the occupation of Francis Owen and his family. Knowing this, Owen immediately set off for Natal to collect his family and his interpreter, a Mr Hulley, and his wife. Their arrival at emGungungdlovi was on 7th October 1837.

The missionary soon sallied forth with bible and books, to give reading lessons to the children of the kraal. To his amazement Dingaan also wanted to learn, and joined the children during their lessons. He soon lost interest though, finding it tedious and hard going, but he never lost his curiosity in the bible and would listen intently as Owen explained the meaning of various bible stories.

In November of that year Dingaan began to have meetings

with Piet Retief, one of the Boer leaders who had always been given a right royal welcome, with feasting, dancing and general merry-making; and of course, the entertainment invariably included warriors doing their various war dances. The first time Retief saw a full Zulu regiment on exercise, he realised the potential of the warriors as a fighting force.

The king watched Retief very keenly while he was watching the dancing, and on one occasion offered to give the Boers a grant of land if they would first do him a favour. This was, to capture a certain Chief Syonkella, who had been raiding the cattle from Zulu territory. Dingaan happened to know that this chief had guns and horses which he also wanted, but he neglected to tell Retief about those. Retief did indeed capture the chief but failed to hand him over to Dingaan, ransoming him instead for cattle and then returning him to his own clan. Dingaan was livid and determined to get his own back. Biding his time for a few weeks, he lulled Retief into a false sense of security, then invited him and all his people on a visit, to officially receive the grant of land on which they could settle. He also told them that he wished to show them a display of horsemanship, and wanted their advice on how to teach the young men of the clan to ride.

Retief accepted the invitation and arrived on 3rd February 1838. The king's speaker (called the mouth) welcomed him and his people on behalf of the king, asking them to camp just outside the royal kraal. He also requested them to lodge their guns in the royal enclosure. Retief said they would stay outside the kraal but would keep their guns!

On the 4th February, Retief and five of his men discussed Dingaan's grant of land with him and it was agreed they could have a huge tract of land in Southern Natal. A document was drawn up, Retief signed it and Dingaan signed it with his mark.

Next day, the 5th, the king arranged a display of two regiments dancing in formation with herds of trained oxen. The first herd were all black, and the first regiment had black shields to match. The other oxen were all white and white shields were held by the second regiment. These regiments were the élite Zulu troops and they all wore the warrior's headband, a circlet of tree-bark and grass stitched through the skin of the scalp.

The Boer party intended to leave on the 6th, but Retief was asked by Dingaan at the last moment to let his people attend a final ceremony before leaving. Being on the point of departure the party was caught completely off guard, having packed all their weapons, but they had the treaty and didn't want to upset the king, so accepted the invitation.

First of all Dingaan wished them well and a safe journey. He further said he hoped they would be very happy in their new territory and then offered them milk and beer to drink. As they relaxed Dingaan asked Retief to sit near him, and the other Boers were placed in positions where they were told they would have a good view of the dancing. Having already had three days of entertainment, no one was unduly worried when the dancers moved in closer to them. They failed to notice the armed Zulu regiment at the back of them.

Suddenly Dingaan jumped to his feet and shouted, "*Babulaleai abathakalthi* (kill the wizards)." The warriors pounced, tied them up and took them away. They were all killed by having their brains beaten out at Homo Amabata (the place of the skulls).

Dingaan then went along to the main body of trekkers, as the Boers were called, and massacred all of them — approximately three hundred — half being children, as well as the same number of coloured workers.

Owen was supposed to have heard of the decision to kill the Boers and was very concerned about his own people, but was assured they would not be harmed. One of the other missionaries, Jane Williams, observed it all from a spot overlooking the royal kraal and was shattered by what she saw. Each Boer was manhandled by about nine or ten Zulu warriors and was dragged to the place of execution before being killed.

The king excused his action by claiming that the Boers had intended to take up arms against him, and he was frightened by their firearms. Owen realised he and his people were in a very perilous position and now had proof that Dingaan wasn't in the least interested in Christianity. He asked the king's permission to leave the mission station, whereupon Dingaan accused him of having sympathy for the Boers; but, nevertheless, he gave his consent.

When Owen was ready to leave he went to the kraal, to find the king surrounded by his councillors and seeming to be very angry. Dingaan told Owen he had found out that he was in league with the Boers. One of Owen's maids was supposed to have reported having heard Owen say that Dingaan was a murderous dog and had called on his God to condemn him. Owen emphatically denied this and asked how his maid could possibly know what he had said, since she could not understand English. Dingaan fortunately conceded this and his anger abated. He then stated that he hadn't really wanted the missionaries there and was glad the mission station was to be vacated. From this time on, it would remain empty. Owen said his farewells and left with his family and servants for Port Natal.

Dingaan now lost all restraint concerning the Boers and on the 15th February 1838, his warriors attacked a trekker group, slaughtering some four hundred men, women and children. This incident sparked off a full-scale war between the Boers and the Zulus. On the 15th December the Boers formed a large laager (camp) at elThaleni (the place of the shelf), near the banks of a stream which was later to bear the name of Blood River.

Instead of the camp being erected in the usual circular fashion, it was triangular in shape. One row of waggons overlooked a fifteen foot high bank, another row skirted a broad, deep stretch of water, while a third faced the open veld, a tract of land, flat and devoid of bush or shrubbery. All the wagons were firmly chained together. Everything was prepared, muzzle-loading firearms were at the ready and ammunition placed near the cannons (small metal gun-barrels mounted on two-wheeled wooden supports, which fired hollow cannon-balls filled with gunpowder, lit by fuses which caused them to burst into fragments on reaching their target). Lanterns were strung along from wagon top to wagon top, to provide light in case the warriors attacked at night.

The Boer's 'scouts' reported the move of the Zulu army toward the camp and the assault was expected before midnight, but nothing happened until daybreak of the 16th December.

The first line of warriors arrived at the camp and the

'heavens' exploded, with all the cannons being fired at once; the guns were being loaded by the women the moment they had been fired, and as each man had two apiece, firing never ceased; consequently, they were never weaponless as Dingaan had supposed. The air was filled with the acrid smell of gunpowder used in the cannons. Zulus were going down like 'ninepins' as they were mown down by the Boer guns on every side.

The remaining Zulus decided to move to safer ground to have a discussion to decide their next plan of action. All of a sudden the second horde rushed onto the camp, and this time the Boers again used all the cannons at once, and then the guns. This decimated most of the warriors and nothing could be seen but mounds of corpses. The River Ncome now became blood red from the dead and dying warriors, who had hurled themselves into it to escape, but the Boers walked along the banks and as soon as a Zulu brought his head out of the water to breathe, he was shot down.

Eventually the remnant of the Zulu army went trailing back to the royal kraal and Dingaan, after such a defeat, was forced to sign an agreement which ended the war, one of the conditions being that the rest of the Zulu people would leave the territory of Natal, which the Boers would then occupy.

At one point during his ignominious retreat, Dingaan looked back and saw smoke rising from the royal kraal, and knew from that moment his reign had come to an end. This was in January 1839.

February 1840 saw the accession to the Zulu throne of Mpanda (the root), another of Dingaan's half-brothers, and one who in his earlier days had been thought of as a half-wit. The Boers placed him on the throne and because of their help, Mpanda gave them many herds of cattle.

Dingaan eventually hid himself in a forest in Swaziland. Blaming Ndlela, his chief warrior, for the defeat at Blood River, he had him strangled and thrown to the beasts of prey, saying he was not fit to be buried as a warrior. This act of cruelty was too much for some of the other chiefs to stomach, and they began to plot Dingaan's assassination. Many others fled to join the new king, Mpanda.

After Ndlela's execution, Dingaan, his people and the few

C

warriors he had left, journeyed eastward through Swaziland, approaching the great Lubombo Mountain, trespassing through the territory of the Nyawo tribe, of whom Silevana was regent. Many members of Silevana's family had been murdered by Dingaan in the past, therefore he was very worried indeed when informed of Dingaan taking possession of a prominent hill named Hlatikhulu (The Great Forest), and had ordered the building of a royal kraal.

Silevana decreed that the Zulu must be dispersed at the first opportunity, and his army proceeded to cause as much harassment to Dingaan and his subjects as possible.

He was eventually killed by a small army of Nyawos, led by Silevana. One morning in early March 1840, the kraal was surrounded. Silevana and three chiefs of the army entered the camp. The people of Dingaan's clan were very frightened and started to run all over the place in their panic, thinking they were to be massacred, but the chiefs assured them they were safe.

Dingaan was awakened by the screaming and noise, and went outside to see what the commotion was about, whereupon he was confronted by Silevana and two chief warriors. Dingaan knew, of course, why they were there and pleaded for his life, but the first spear went through his side, the second felled him and the third was plunged straight through his body. His murder was almost a replica of his brother Chaka's.

After his death, Silevana had a hole dug into which Dingaan's corpse was placed, branches of the very thorny mphafa tree were then cut to cover the top of the hole and three heavy, large stones finally covered the top to hold everything down.

So ended the life of another tyrant Zulu king.

Chapter 5

Mpanda — the new king

A few months before his death, after the conflict with the Boers, Dingaan had launched a campaign against the Swazi tribe, which he lost. He blamed his defeat on his brother Mpanda, who everyone had thought to be a half-wit. Dingaan had only let him live because of this belief, as he hadn't seen him as a threat or possible rival to himself.

The reason Dingaan thought he had lost the battle through Mpanda's fault was that Mpanda was supposed to send a supporting force, but because of his hatred for Dingaan and his dislike of warfare, he didn't do so. Dingaan was livid and said that Mpanda was to be captured and killed.

For ten years, Mpanda had been leading a very indolent, comfortable and even luxurious life, becoming extremely fat. He was an introvert and stayed very much in the background; in fact, many Zulu clans didn't even know of his existence. His own clan absolutely adored him, as he was only interested in their welfare. The women of his seraglio couldn't do enough for him, as he was such a kind and considerate man.

After Dingaan's defeat at the hands of the Swazis, he heard the rumours of his possible capture and death and became very frightened. He had a talk with his councillors and it was decided the whole clan, with their cattle, would go to Natal. He told his people that he would not stand in their way if they wanted to join Dingaan; needless to say, not many did so!

In September 1839 Mpanda and approximately 17,000 set out on the journey. Travelling in single file, which became known as Mpanda's Rope, they arrived in Natal where they were challenged by a Boer hunting party. Mpanda asked them if they would take him to Pietermaritzburg to have a talk with Andreis Pretorius* (a Boer patriot who led the early settlers in their war with the Zulus) and the Volksraad (folks' council), a legislative assembly special to the Transvaal, or Orange Free State, before 1900. It assumed absolute control over the church, the local government and all other functions of local government, and it appointed the local magistrate and wardmasters, who were directly responsible to the Volksraad for their actions.

At his interview in October, Mpanda was able to convince the council of his peaceful intentions, and asked for land whereon he and his people could settle. He offered to send out his scouts to see if they could find out what Dingaan was up to and where he might be hiding, also how large a fighting force he still possessed. Pretorius loaned them some land in the area of the Thongani River until Dingaan was completely routed, when Mpanda could go back to Zululand. Meanwhile, on his return to the tribe, his people immediately set to and built a royal kraal which he called Mahambehlala (the wanderers' rest). The amazing thing was, he now became energetic enough to help to build it, and also began discussions with his chiefs on how to help in the overthrow of Dingaan.

When the Boers realised what an honest, nice man he was, they crowned him reigning prince of the emigrant Zulus. This was at the end of October 1839. The other chiefs who had fled from Dingaan previously, were so pleased, they came forward and offered the Boers their support in invading Zululand.

When at last the opposing Zulus had been defeated, Pretorius and the Volksraad went to see Mpanda to thank him for his loyalty. They also praised his chiefs for their generalship, and at the same time thanked the other chiefs, Matuwane and Jobe. To Mpanda's delight they told him of Dingaan's flight into foreign territory, and of their decision to proclaim him (Mpanda) King of the Zulu, in place of the deposed Dingaan.

Mpanda pledged his undying loyalty to Pretorius and to the white government, offering to give assistance at any time. His reign was to prove peaceful and prosperous. He had no

*Pretoria, in the Transvaal, was named after him.

grandiose plans for expansion and besides, although he was now king, he was under the jurisdiction of the Boer republic.

This was the first time for years that the Zulu nation was at peace. They were able to go back to their first love, the land — sowing seeds, planting trees and generally getting back to a completely pastoral life. Mpanda reigned for thirty-two years, most of which were uneventful. It was therefore a shock, when in 1850 civil war broke out in Zululand and most of his subjects were massacred. He lived on in abject misery, being unable to walk because of his massive weight, due again to his indolent life and over-feasting. He became a very sick and unhappy man, both mentally and physically. He died in 1872 and was buried in his capital kraal, Nodwengu.

In 1873 his son Cetewayo officially ruled. He was made of sterner stuff, and recreated a strong army once more, but in 1878 Zululand was annexed by the British, and the Zulu nation was completely crushed in October 1879. During Cetewayo's reign, two battles of note took place — Rorke's Drift in early 1879, and Ulundi in the same year — which led to the downfall of the Zulus as a nation.

The name of Rorke's Drift originated from one of the early settlers named James Rorke. He served as a private in an Irish regiment that landed at Mosselbaai in 1842, to fight against the Kaffirs (a long-forgotten clash). Rorke had either deserted or retired from the army, and decided to remain in Cape Colony. He married and had a son, James, born in 1827, who later served as a civilian with the commissariat in the seventh Kaffir war of 1846.

James married and bought a 3,000 acre farm on the banks of the Buffels River, within ten miles to the east of the Nguti range of mountains. Near the farmhouse he built a small shop in which he bartered or traded goods. To enable his trade to flourish, he knocked down part of the river banks to make a ford. Many hunters, traders and natives used this crossing and it gradually became known as 'Rorke's Drift'.

Several years of misunderstandings and difficulties between the government in London, their officials in Natal and the Zulu nation caused the Zulu War, Rorke's Drift being a resounding victory for the Zulu's, and Ulundi their death knell.

After Cetewayo was captured he was shipped to Cape Town and taken to the old castle, where he was kept in close confinement for fourteen months. In January 1881 he was moved to Oude Moulen, a farm in the suburbs, allowed to have friends and visitors and also to go for country walks. Two of his visitors were Prince Albert and Prince George (the future King George V), who were midshipmen serving on HMS *Bacchante*.

Cetewayo, through Samuelson his interpreter, had been writing many letters to Queen Victoria asking for a sympathetic hearing. In May 1882 he was informed that he would be taken to London to plead his cause, eventually arriving in July and living in a rented house in Kensington.

A few days after his arrival he was invited by Queen Victoria to have lunch with her at Osborne House. Finally he met Lord Kimberley of the colonial office, on 7th August. He received a very sympathetic hearing, with Kimberley promising him generous terms. Cetewayo left England before any details had been settled, but he trusted Kimberley to work out the size of his intended sanctuary territory.

When Cetewayo eventually received the results of the settlement he was devastated, as it bore no relation to the liberal terms which Kimberley had outlined to him; he had no option but to accept, and signed the proposals presented to him, in order to avoid being exiled.

From 1883 Cetewayo suffered setback after setback from his own people, as very few chieftains of other kraals or clans were anxious to be his friends, and the respect he had once enjoyed was now lost.

Many clan clashes now erupted and the Natal authorities blamed the Zulu king and decided to arrest him. Cetewayo fled and took refuge with a friendly chieftain at Gpikazi kraal, where he died a few days later. A messenger was sent to Osborne, one of the Natal officials who had been sent to arrest him, to let him know that the Zulu king was dead and lying in one of their huts. Osborne left with a medical officer, but they realised that Cetewayo had been dead many hours. Although the medical officer certified he had died from 'fatty degeneration of the heart', many people thought he had probably been poisoned!

Cetewayo's eldest son who was only fifteen years old, now took over; his name was Dinezulu. The Afrikaners helped him and named him the Paramount Chief of the Zulus, they also gave him a large district in north-west Zululand. A new republic was now formed and he was able to claim overall control of Zululand, except for the Zulu reserve next to Natal. Britain recognised the New Republic in 1886, but the following year it ceased to exist as it became part of the Transvaal. Dinezulu tried to resist all the new changes which gradually whittled away his power, but it was no good and he was later arrested and exiled to St Helena. When he returned in 1897 it was as headman in the Usutu district. By 1908 the Zulu nation ceased to exist, as over the years they had been beaten by ruthlessness and systematic domination; but even now they are spoken and written about because of their earlier identity and unity, which Chaka had forged.

Chapter 6

*Pietermaritzburg —
city of my birth*

This city, lying in a hollow and surrounded on all sides by hills, is actually the capital of the province of Natal. In October 1838, the Council of the Voortrekkers decided to establish the town and named it Pietermaritzburg in honour of Piet Retief, their former governor, and Gert Maritz, the late president of the council. It wasn't until 1839, after Commander General A.W.J. Pretorius had obtained a decisive victory over Dingaan's impis (regiments), that the voortrekkers felt safe enough to take their final journey to the new town.

Before doing anything else the Volksraad (People's Council) was to survey the town and publish regulations concerning property rights. One of the first laid down was that each piece of land should be allotted to the claimant according to number, or by drawing the lot; at the same time a block of land could be acquired for a family group.

All property owners, apart from minor rules and regulations, had to share the cost of constructing the water-course from the Little Bushman's River (the Dorp Spruit), a tributary of the Umsindusi, to the town. They had to promise to cultivate their land and to build substantial dwelling-houses within three years on the street sides.

The town itself extended about one and a half miles in length and a mile across, divided by eight parallel streets, all of the same width, with a central block left out as a market place.

As the Zulu menace wasn't quite over a church was the first building to be erected, and in April 1840 a wall was built around it to act as a fortification in case of a sudden attack. This had been built at the lower end of the market. The

40

Volksraad Chamber was placed on the north-west corner, and the gaol was built on the north-east corner. Above the town a powder magazine was erected in 1840, by the Volksraad, on a hill which was later known as Fort Napier.

In May 1842, Captain Smith in command of an expeditionary detachment of the 27th Regiment, arrived at Port Natal with instructions to take possession of the port on behalf of the British Government. The Republican Government strongly resisted this action and Captain Smith was besieged for a month. In June of that year two ships arrived, the *Conch* and the *Southampton*, with several more companies of the 27th on board under Colonel A.J. Cloete. Captain Smith was relieved and Commandant General Pretorius and his members of the council, evacuated the port and took up their position in the vicinity of Pietermaritzburg. Colonel Cloete visited the capital early in July 1843, and obtained the submission of the Volksraad and its members.

Henry Cloete had been appointed Her Majesty's Commissioner for Natal, and he arrived to take up residence in June 1843. For good measure two companies of the 45th Regiment pitched their tents on the hill to the west of the town, and named it Fort Napier in honour of Sir George Napier, governor of the Cape of Good Hope.

The Volksraad still continued to function under the supervision of Henry Cloete until October 1845. Natal had by then become a district of the Cape Colony, and a lieutenant general was appointed who also resided in Pietermaritzburg, in a cottage looking over the square.

In 1853 Pietermaritzburg was given the title of city; a year later it was proclaimed a borough and divided into four wards, and the first municipal council came into existence. The first Natal newspaper, *De Natalier*, was published on the 5th April 1844 in Pietermaritzburg. By this time they really felt on top of the world, but they felt extremely proud in 1856 when Natal was created a separate colony by royal charter, and in the following year the first legislative council of the colony was established in Pietermaritzburg, which meant it had the right to be called the capital city.

The opening of the railway in 1880 did away with the old transport riders, as communications were now so much easier.

By 1895 the main line to Johannesburg had been extended and completed, a distance of approximately 300 miles.

The name Natal was given to this area as it was discovered on Christmas Day 1497 — Christ's Natal Day. It achieved its own self-government in July 1893, and joined the Union of South Africa in May 1910.

Before finishing the chapter on Pietermaritzburg I must make a passing reference to a plaque in St Mary's Catholic Church, which bears the following inscription: *Within this building lay in state June 8th-9th 1879, the body of the Prince Imperial of France, killed whilst serving with the British Army in Zululand.*

Prince Louis was a member of Lord Chelmsford's staff during the Zulu War of 1879. He had ridden out with seven companions and a Zulu guide to reconnoitre the area between Blood River and Itelizi Hill, when they were surprised by a group of Zulus, who killed three of the party, one of them being the prince. When found by the search-party he was naked, except for a thin gold chain with a medallion of the Virgin Mary, and his great uncle's (Napoleon Bonaparte) seal around his neck, there were seventeen assegai wounds in his body!

The Zulus were very upset when they heard who they had killed and asked, as a mark of their esteem and respect, to be allowed to be responsible for the upkeep of the memorial stone which had been erected at the spot where he fell.

His body was taken to England on HMS *Orontes* and landed at Woolwich, where the coffin was transferred onto a gun-carriage and drawn to Chislehurst. He was given a military funeral and laid to rest beside his father, Napoleon III.

Chapter 7

My grandfather

I suppose my birth in a foreign country was due to my having had an adventurous grandfather. He was born in North Devon of yeoman stock and was the youngest of four brothers and two sisters. They all wanted to travel, so it was no surprise to their parents when three of their sons became sheep farmers in New Zealand, and their two daughters also went abroad: one to America and the other to South Africa.

Their youngest son, my grandfather, being the baby of the family, had to stay at home, but as soon as he was eighteen years old his parents allowed him to go to Canada, as that was the place he wished to see most. His main ambition at that time was to learn to be a trapper and to do so under his own steam.

It was in 1880 that he worked his passage on a tramp steamer and joined a group of Cree indians, who were noted trappers of their day. He thoroughly enjoyed living with the tribe and grew to have a great respect for them and their knowledge of tracking, trapping and skinning. The furs were usually sold to the Hudson's Bay Company, which was a company formed in 1670 for this specific purpose.

The Hudson's Bay Company derived its name from a certain Henry Hudson, who had sailed into this vast inland ocean in the early 1600s, while looking for a north-west passage to the Pacific.

Grandfather stayed just over a year with the indians, but developed itchy feet once again and decided to head for Alaska. Why Alaska? Well, when he was three years old, the USA had just bought the country from the Russians for one and a half million dollars, and he had listened to his parents discussing the deal, learning that most Americans had been very much opposed to the idea and had thought William Henry Seward (secretary of state) mad to even think of buying such a barren place of useless glaciers and frozen waste. They had called it 'Seward's folly'. How wrong they were, as it was to prove a very great asset indeed, especially as in 1890 gold was discovered, together with many other minerals. The gold alone covered the cost of the land many times over. The other minerals included copper, silver, lead, tin and of course marble, which is quarried up in the rocky hills.

As Grandfather felt he was experienced enough to trap and skin animals on his own account, he set out with a friend to become a trapper once again. They first made their way to Juneau which was Alaska's gold-rush capital, but not being interested in the gold, they went on further afield to the forests, where they knew foxes, wolves, polar bears and many small 'furry' animals could be found. They were mostly concerned with fox furs, which were their main source of income, and they were always welcomed with open arms at the various trading posts along the way, all of which traded in furs. The more full your saddle-bags were, the more welcome you were.

I have wished many times that I could have been with him to see (as he said) 'ice and water glistening like steel in the distance', and 'the lush forest greenery covered in a blue haze which gave it a lovely soft, shimmery sheen.' He was quite fascinated by the forests, where great hemlock trees — so called because their branches are supposed to resemble hemlock leaves — spruce, and of course the Alaska red cedars, all grew in profusion. The Alaskan mountain ranges too were one of his everlasting loves, as he could never forget their great height and rugged faces. As he said, they made him feel so small in such an insignificant part of the world.

He spent two years out there altogether and only came home because he suddenly realised how homesick he felt. Once again working his passage, he returned to his parents' farm on the outskirts of Crediton, North Devon, but had only been home about two months when a letter arrived from a friend, inviting him to go whaling. Grandfather was delighted, as this was something else he had dreamed of doing.

Off he went to join a fleet which was sailing for Antarctic waters. Many such voyages in those days lasted anything up to five years, but this one only lasted for eighteen months which was just as well, since Grandfather was disgusted and sickened by the destruction of these splendid animals. So much so, that he vowed never again would he hurt, maim or kill any of God's creatures.

On returning to England, he felt ready for a more peaceful existence and thought it would be nice to visit his brothers in New Zealand, to find out, by working for them for a while, whether he too would like to become a sheep farmer. In any case, it would be nice to have a look at that part of the Commonwealth.

Making his way to Southampton, he was lucky enough to be taken on as one of the crew by the captain of a liner that was calling in at New Zealand. Although having no desire to be a sailor, he nevertheless always enjoyed working aboard any kind of boat that was going in the right direction.

Whilst staying with his brothers and learning about sheep farming, he found the animals were bred mostly for export, which meant them being slaughtered. This wasn't for him; but one thing he found which did have a great appeal: all his brothers were married and had children.

He had a sudden yen to get married to 'the girl he'd left behind' and settle down to family life. He was well able to afford a wife, having made sufficient money in the fur trade through shrewdness, together with a brilliant business brain, which enabled him to make many profitable deals.

Wanting his brothers to attend the wedding, he sent for his fiancée who lived in the village of Hartland, North Devon, to join him, also arranging that she travel out with her parents and her future mother and father-in-law. His two sisters were also able to attend, which meant he had the blessing of the whole family. The marriage took place in the Parish of Christchurch in 1885, and Father was born in the same city eighteen months later.

Being a parent made grandfather realize he had responsibilities and his roving life had to stop. He decided therefore to return to England with his wife and son, in order to collect the considerable amount of money his father had been setting aside for him during the years he had spent abroad.

Several months after they had returned to England they were invited to go and stay with Grandfather's sister, who lived in Durban, South Africa. So, saying goodbye to parents and friends they once again set sail for foreign parts.

It was while staying with her that he bought a tea plantation, and grocery and provision shop. By late 1889 he was well and truly established as a merchant trader, and formed his own company. Fourteen years later he had a chain of grocery and provision shops in various towns in South Africa, such as Cape Town, Durban, East London, Johannesburg and Pietermaritzburg, where he could market his own tea from the plantation.

Chapter 8

My parents — Mother's death and burial at sea — Father's death on armistice day

Father was just over two years old when his parents went to South Africa, and he spent the next fourteen years out there before returning to England in order to finish his education at the London University. (I have been unable to ascertain whether or not he attained any degrees from there.) Two years later he entered the Royal Academy of Music, where he succeeded in becoming a Licentiate of the Royal Academy (LRAM) and an associate of same (ARAM). He was later to be employed in South Africa, by the academy, to audition talented young pianists and violinists to see if they were good enough to be admitted as students.

While living in London he spent his holidays in Cardiff with a merchant friend of his father's, who had two daughters, one of whom was only a few months older than himself, and he became very fond of her. It came as no surprise to her parents, when he was on one of these holidays, that he asked for their daughter's hand in marriage. They were allowed to become engaged, but he had to finish his education and return to South Africa to spend a couple of years with his father in the business, learning to be a merchant buyer. Therefore the young couple had to bide their time and be satisfied with letter writing.

A couple of months before Father was due to travel to England for his wedding, he was very ill with pneumonia and the doctor had advised him to stay in England for several months to convalesce. So after he and Mother were married at the Methodist Church, Roath Park, Cardiff, in October 1911, they went to live at Kisber, Queen's Avenue, Church End,

47

Finchley, N., from where Father was able to continue his work as a buyer for the firm and to accept various musical engagements at soirées or concert halls.

My brother Deryck was born there in 1913. When he was four months old, Father decided he felt fit enough to travel and live in Pietermaritzburg, South Africa, once again; and I, of course, was born there in 1915.

Soon after my birth Father was ill again, this time with malaria, and the doctor advised him to go back to England to recuperate. They thought it a marvellous idea, especially Mother, as she was anxious to show off her new baby girl (myself). Arrangements were made for us to travel on one of the Union Castle liners, *The Kenilworth Castle*, one of two ships which had been ordered for the Cape trade in 1900. With the outbreak of war in 1914 she was commandeered in Cape Town as a transport liner, which meant she conveyed home a portion of the imperial garrison stationed in South Africa. From January 1915 she was used as a mail ship, and sailed as often as possible under wartime conditions. This was the ship we sailed on in October 1915.

After a few days on board, Mother and Father started to organise concerts and various other entertainments for the troops, and being singers and pianists, were able to do some of the entertaining themselves. Father was also a violinist and well known orchestral conductor, so his services were in great demand.

All was well on the voyage until Mother suddenly developed blood poisoning through, it was said, pricking a pimple on her lip. The attack became so virulent that an operation had to be performed by the ship's doctor, assisted by the army doctors. This took place on 29th October, but she died on the 30th, leaving my father completely grief-stricken. She was buried at sea, an hour's journey north of Teneriffe. Two beautiful wreaths were made by the passengers and troops, and these tributes were lowered into the water with her body. My father received many letters of sympathy from passengers, troops, and from the ship's officers, who referred to the appreciation of the whole ship's company for the efforts made by Mother to entertain the troops aboard.

Father stayed in England for four months, convalescing

from his illness and recovering from his great and sudden loss. We returned to South Africa to live in Durban, in February 1916. After Mother's death he never really regained his health, and any minor illness was apt to weaken him still further. In July 1918 he developed pneumonia, and although he recovered, he was never quite fit; therefore it was no surprise to anyone when he contracted Spanish flu, of which there was a world-wide epidemic at that time. It was responsible for millions of deaths. Father died at the age of thirty years, on 11th November 1918, Armistice Day. The Spanish flu was generally thought to have originated from the thousands of dead bodies left unburied on the battlefields of France, during the 1914-1918 war.

This meant I first learnt of death at the tender age of 3½. I distinctly remember being picked up and placed on the bed where my father lay dying, and being told to 'kiss Papa goodbye, as he was going on a long journey to meet Jesus and live with him up in the sky'.

No one, at that time, knew the effect this had on me and it wasn't until later, whilst living with my grandparents, that they realised that something was wrong. I used to start screaming whenever I saw them leaving the house, as I thought that they *too* were going on a long journey and I would never see them again.

Father was buried at St Andrew's Presbyterian Church in Commercial Road, Durban, where, at the time of his death, he was the organist. The officiating minister was his grandfather, who had been the minister there for many years. Members of the Durban Railway Band attended, as Father had been their founder and band-master. Many people, well known in Durban musical circles, also attended — they had all been friends and associates of my father.

After the funeral, my grandparents took Deryck and I to live with them on the outskirts of Doonside, where Grandfather had his tea plantation. Many years later he adopted us as his own children.

D

Chapter 9

Sixpence (Sipho) and village (kraal) life

The first person I met on arrival at Grandfather's house in Doonside was Sixpence (I never knew whether it was a nickname or a translation of his real name), the aged 'houseboy' who opened the door for us. He was very tall, I should think about 6ft 4in., slim and dressed in immaculate shorts and jacket, which was the uniform of houseboys — and of course they all had bare feet.

Although there was an Indian ayah (children's nurse) to look after us, I always seemed to follow Sixpence about, listening to his stories of kraal life. I was even allowed, with Grandfather's permission, to go and play with his numerous grandchildren in his kraal, which was near the bottom of our garden.

Before the Zulus were finally defeated by the British, Sixpence had been a tribal chief. These chiefs were always direct descendants of the dead (or deposed) chief, who would be elected (if his dying father had not been able, for some reason or other, to nominate him) by the head warriors of the various clans. Although the tribal chief was all-powerful, if he didn't rule justly his subjects would desert him and join a new clan with a more friendly and just ruler.

The tribal chief was the 'father of his tribe' and upheld its traditions, laws, and way of life. His position, rather than his personality, claimed by right the loyalty of his people. He was assisted by a council, mainly nominated by him, to help maintain the unwritten traditions of the tribe; which included such things as justice, land, grazing and watering rights, also family squabbles.

Before a youth became a man he had to be initiated into

manhood, which was called the ceremony of Abakwetha, lasting for three months. Normally only four or five youths took part at one time, and the first thing to happen was for them to wear calabashes (the dried shell of the gourd) over their private parts. Women were only allowed to see them like that, but two weeks before the actual ceremony, they were painted completely white from head to foot to prove (symbolically) that the complexion of youth changes to that of manhood only after circumcision.

They remained like that for three months, all the time being counselled by the witch-doctor's assistant, who taught them the rights and duties of manhood. During this time they lived in a circular hut which the men of the tribe built and the women thatched. The initiates, after their heads had been shaved clean, moved into the hut, which was well away from the village and there they stayed until their ordeal was over.

The circumcision took place in the second month and was performed by the witch-doctor himself. He didn't use anaesthetics but had herbs to stop the bleeding and act as antiseptic. When the incision was made the youth would cry out, "I am a man." For a week afterwards he had to eat and drink without either food or water touching his hands. He also had to show he was strong enough to go without, so he used a skewer to stick in the meat and transfer it to his mouth, chewed it and then spat it out, doing exactly the same with drinks, even his beer. When the week was over, he could eat and drink normally.

To keep track of time they cut notches in a piece of stick, to denote how many days they had spent in the hut. A month after the circumcision they dressed up in skirts, either made of grass or leaves, and donned most magnificent head-dresses. They were now ready to dance the ceremonial dance and all the village turned out to give them encouragement, chanting and beating on drums.

While the dance was being held, a herd of cattle would be driven down to the river-bank. As the young men had to bathe after the ceremony to wash off the paint, in order to cover their nakedness they would walk back to the hut among the animals. On arrival back at the hut they were rubbed with ox fat until their skin glistened. They would then be seen sitting outside the hut making a sidal (a pouch) of sheepskin, with which to cover their genitals!

The hut was then burnt down, the young men daubed their bodies with red clay and were given the traditional blanket. They were now considered to be men and eligible for marriage, so a great feast was held with much merry-making and drinking, while they were given many presents and much advice by the other men of the village.

Girls also had an initiation ceremony to undergo, but it wasn't as gruelling and only lasted a week. First of all they were taken down to the river and washed by the older women of the clan. A goat was killed and its raw skin used for the girls to sleep on during the week. They lived in a hut which was situated out of sight of the other huts. The flesh of the goat was cooked and used for a feast, during which goat's milk was also drunk.

On the last day of the initial ceremony a witch-doctor entered the hut and ceremonially tattooed the girls with black beauty spots and lucky symbols all over their bodies. Afterwards they showed themselves and were then, like the men, considered ready for marriage and could be wed as soon as a man could pay the bride price.

When a man had chosen his bride, and the young couple wished to get married, her father would ask so many cattle as her dowry — the prettier the girl, the more animals he could ask for. The giving of cattle was supposed to bind a couple legally and if, for any reason, the wife left the husband, the father would receive his dowry back; but he could only then justify keeping them if the wife could prove she had been so badly treated that she'd had no option but to run away.

The night before the wedding the bride-to-be, often with seventy to a hundred of her people, arrived within sight of her future bridegroom's kraal shortly before sunset. They would seat themselves on the hill nearest to the village and there they would wait until someone from the kraal went out to escort them to the hut, in which food had been prepared for their coming. It was usually the old men who went out to bid them welcome, and they would be ushered in with great ceremony and words of encouragement to the bride, who was supposed to keep on weeping to show her unhappiness at having to leave her own clan.

The next day, with her bridesmaids, she would go to the river to be prepared for her wedding. Her hair was done up in a top-knot and plastered together with clay, her face would be covered either in a veil, or beaded ornaments, she would wear a cowhide skirt which came to her knees, and bead necklaces, in such profusion that they covered her breasts.

When they were ready, which would be a little before noon, the bridal party would start to sing and dance on their way to the bridegroom's kraal. Arriving there the bride would be encircled by her friends and the groom would emerge also surrounded by his friends. The marriage ceremony was deemed complete when the groom's friends managed to manoeuvre the bride into their circle. You can imagine the noise and happy laughter that went on during this boisterous struggle, and the cheers that went up when she was finally standing next to her husband. As soon as this had been achieved, all of his friends would pass before her, extolling his virtues and telling her what a lucky girl she was, and how fortunate for her that she has entered such a noble family and how unworthy she was for such an honour!

Mind you, it wasn't all one-sided, as the bride's friends were doing exactly the same thing to the groom, and in no uncertain terms letting him know how unworthy he was to have such a busy, industrious, and thrifty girl as his wife!

Then the feasting began and everyone except the bride enjoyed it. The poor bride had to cry, weep and wail to show her unhappiness at leaving home and, to add to her miseries, she was not allowed to eat anything, as that would be an insult to her own people and prove that she wasn't really unhappy.

Sixpence told me that he had been married like that and how frightened he had felt at assuming the mantle of a married man and having a girl from another clan as his wife. Fortunately they were very, very happy together and had a large family of six sons and three daughters. The children were themselves all married, with sons and daughters of their own. These were the children I was allowed to play with.

The older men of the kraal worked on Grandfather's tea plantation, whilst the younger ones were our houseboys and were being trained by Sixpence in their various duties. When

Sixpence had finished his work he would go straight to his hut in the kraal, take off his uniform and don his native dress, which consisted of a thick skirt of fringe made from twisted strips of skin with hair or fur left on, which just covered his loins; and of course he covered himself completely with the blanket, which he had been given after his initiation into manhood.

Occasionally he would put on his ceremonial regalia, just to let us see how magnificent he looked as a warrior. His war kilt was knee-length and made from rolled civet, genet (similar to a cat) and monkey skins. His arms and legs were decorated with ox-tail tufts, and a broad ruffle of ox-hide protected his ankles from getting scratched or cut by thorns or stones. He also wore bead ornaments and a necklace of horns with small pieces of wood interspersed amongst them, which meant he had excelled in battles; but you should have seen his magnificent head-dress which was made up of a variety of pelts, decorated with gay tail plumes and breast feathers of exotic birds.

The huts in the kraal were very spacious and warm. They were built by driving long flexible sticks into the ground and curving them to the required height, which was usually seven to eight feet, forming a rounded top. They then neatly wove other flexible sticks and reeds through them and when that was done, the whole thing was thatched over with grass. The inside was plastered with dung from their animals, mixed with clay. It was smeared on the walls and floor to strengthen it. The doorway was shaped like an arch and was the only opening in the hut.

As I have mentioned in the brief history of the Zulu, these huts were built in a circular pattern around a cattle-fold, where there was plenty of water, which made the land very fertile and very good pasture for cattle-grazing.

During the day, the grandsons of Sixpence looked after the herd, taking them out to graze and keeping a sharp look-out for wild animals, which might be hungry. During the night they were, of course, kept safe in the centre of the huts.

As Sixpence was the patriarch of his kraal he had the biggest and best of the huts, where he lived with his mother and first wife. The other huts were inhabited by his married sons and their children. Sixpence also had two other wives and they each had their own hut in which they brought up his other children.

The grandmother was the most popular member of the family as, after the evening meal, they would sit in a circle round the open hearth beside the huts, while she regaled them with age-old folk stories. She would bring to life the daring exploits of heroes of bygone days, and tell of the legend of how death came into the world. It happened thus: the first man who trod the earth found himself in a bed of reeds beside the river. A spirit told a lizard to tell the man he might live for ever, then the spirit sent for a chameleon and told him to tell the man he must die. The lizard rushed off at a cracking pace but fell asleep on the way, while the chameleon just plodded along steadily and was first to reach the man with the message of death!

I learnt many things at the kraal and was allowed to join in with some, such as dancing with the children when they were learning the Zulu war dance. I was dressed in a leopardskin and held a leopardskin shield in my hand, while I danced in my bare feet like the other children, to the chanting and thudding of the drums. Most of the Zulu dances told of various wars which had been won by their brave warriors. The dances themselves consisted of much shuffling of the feet, bending of the knees and leaping into the air, while trying to twirl and twist the body at the same time.

Most of the Zulus I spoke to answered me in what was known as 'Pidgin English' — a jargon mainly consisting of the English and Afrikaans language. They did in fact have their own language, which sounded lovely and was called the 'Washo Alphabet'. It was supposed to be grammatically perfect and could be written as clearly and fully as any European language. The vocabulary was more than twice as large as that used by the peasants of England in olden days. When they talked to each other you could sometimes hear 'clicks', which came into the alphabet in certain words. The language is to South Africa as Latin is to Europe.

I loved to watch the women of the kraal pounding the hard maize corn into powder, which they did by scattering the seeds onto a large flat stone, then rolling a round stone over them again and again, until it had the powdered thickness required for cooking (coarse for a flat bread and very fine for porridge). The stones were supposed to contain iron and it was believed they transferred some of the metal's beneficial qualities to the flour. It was hard work and they used to laugh at me whenever I tried to do it. Most Zulu meals were made with this maize (called mealies), and the women knew up to nineteen different ways to cook it, using either milk or curdled milk. It was the mainstay of their diet.

When the maize was ready for harvesting, as it would not be used for some time, it was stored in a grain pit. These were always dug very deeply, in dry places where the rain could easily run off. The hole was small at the top, bulged out at the sides, and was smaller again at the bottom — somewhat like a bottle. The ground was raised round its mouth and was then smeared and made hard, and a large flat stone was used to cover the top. Apart from keeping the maize dry, it kept out the air and seemed to keep it very fresh. The inside walls were also smeared, pounded hard and made smooth in order to keep the grain safe from weevils and other insects. These pits could hold two to three hundred bushels of grain, and when empty were used as good-sized rooms, if you were small enough to get through the mouth.

The women of Sixpence's kraal, apart from working hard in the village and looking after their families, also did our laundry. They used to take the dirty clothes down to the river and slap them on the big broad stones, which were half-submerged in the water. It was wonderful to watch them and to listen to them singing and laughing while they worked. When the clothes were considered to be clean enough they were gathered together, and with two women to each article, they were spread out on the trees and bushes and left to dry in the blazing sun. You have never seen such dazzling white clothes in all your life.

The men used to look after the breeding and health of their cattle and were also hunters, craftsmen and artisans. Their bead and basketwork was so beautiful, it was considered a work of art. It depended on the sequence in which the colours and design of the beadwork were worked, as to which story of the many Zulu heroes was being depicted.

Cattle breeding, though, was the main occupation of the men, as it was the very life-blood of the tribe. The milk and curdled milk kept the women happy, as milk was the staple diet of the tribe, and the hides were made into war shields, thongs, karosses (South African skin blankets), floor mats, bags, drums, and clothing. The broad horns of the cows were longer than four feet from tip to tip, and these were made into drinking vessels, various other utensils and musical horns.

I remember hearing a story about a lady whose field-boys looked after her animals, and were having trouble getting a new calf away from its mother and into the stable. She walked a little way towards a large log of wood, to pick it up for protection, when all of a sudden the cow turned her head, left the boys and made straight for her. She stood completely still, not realising what was happening, but hoping as the animal got nearer that the horns would hit the log and only its nose hit her. This in fact actually happened, but unfortunately she fell and was kicked and trampled on by the cow. The boys managed to beat it off but the woman was very, very shocked by the event, and although she was up and about in a couple of months she never really got over it.

Cattle hides were made into skirts for the women. Unmarried girls only wore a skirt, but a blouse was added after they were married, when only the husband and babies were allowed to see their breasts. The married women also wore an 'isidwaba' — a very wide skirt heavily smeared with fat, in order to soften the hide and to help keep the pleats in. When they moved away from the fire in winter, they would don a blanket as a cloak.

Cattle were never killed for food unless it was to be used for a sacrifice, such as a funeral, when an oxen would be used and its carcass offered to the shades of the dead.

Zulu funerals were very systematic and were conducted in a very orderly manner. The grave was dug so that the body would be in a sitting position, facing east. Blankets, mats etc. which belonged to the dead person were also put into the grave, to keep his spirit warm (if it was a man being buried his war weapons would be given to his eldest son). Mats were then placed all over; the grave was then filled in with earth and carefully watched over for several days.

Prayers of thanksgiving and repentance were delivered to the Supreme Being, Nkulunkulu (the Great Great One) at the same time as the offering of the sacrifice. They also believed that the spirits of their ancestors hovered about them on earth, and if someone was taken ill they would think that the ancestor was hungry, or displeased, so they made the sacrifice in order to appease him. Raw meat was left in an empty hut overnight and the next day friends of the sick person would take the meat, cook it and have quite a feast!

Not far from the kraal was a narrow pathway which was shaded by trees and surrounded by green hills, covered with a profusion of beautifully coloured flowers which ran right down to the edge of some water, coming from a little stream that gurgled over the rocks. Many of the most colourful flowers were completely scentless, while the smaller plain ones, were very, very fragrant indeed. One day I was walking along the pathway with some Zulu children when we suddenly heard in the distance an old Zulu war song, being sung in perfect harmony by about sixty people who were living in a nearby kraal. I can remember the sound vividly to this day, it was quite beautiful.

Before leaving the kraal I must tell you that the Zulus were a very proud and courteous race and as far as the children were concerned, extremely polite. They would, under no circumstances, interrupt while their elders were speaking. If a Zulu boy fell over and hurt himself, his father would say to him, "You must not scream or make a fuss as you are a little Zulu man," but the funny thing was that if I fell and hurt myself, Sixpence, in spite of his great height, would kneel on the floor, smack it hard and say, *"Voetsak diablo,"* which if I remember correctly, meant 'get away you devil, for hurting missey'.

My grandfather had a great love for the family of the kraal, and he would tell me that when a Zulu was properly treated he would work for the same family for years, as such an honest and trustworthy people would be considered part of the family. No wonder I loved being with Sixpence and his family. I felt and still feel extremely honoured that they allowed me to become part of their lives.

Chapter 10

Doonside — the house on the top of the hill

The house which stood on the top of the hill at Doonside was to be my home for the next four years (Sixpence lived in the kraal, which was situated on the bank of the River Doon, about twenty minutes' walk from the house). It stood there in all its glory, overlooking the Atlantic Ocean and the main shipping route to England. The front garden stretched down to the beach in three tiers. The first tier was a most beautiful green lawn, leading to the second of fragrant, exotic flowers, brilliantly coloured, and the third tier was covered with fruit bushes, especially Cape gooseberries (which have a most exquisite taste), small and yellow with a rather thin transparent skin, completely different from the English variety. This third tier also had a small gate which led directly onto the beach.

The house itself was built on legs which were about three feet in height (this was to allow any creepy-crawly, slithering creatures, such as snakes, to have right of way but no access to the house). The building itself was very spacious and airy and had a veranda running completely around it. All the doors opened onto it, which gave access to the house without using the front door. The two toilets, though, were outside and about ten minutes walk from the back door. This was because of the heat and no plumbing systems to flush away the sewage. We were far too far away from civilisation to have any niceties of that sort (about 200 miles from Cape Town).

The toilets were like small huts, with a wooden seat running the complete width, at the back, with a hole cut out in the middle on which you sat. Under the hole was a large bucket, which was changed very, very early in the morning before anyone was about by a low caste Indian, whom most people ignored if they saw him, as he was thought to be the lowest of the low. I always felt very sorry for him having to be on his own and doing such a dirty job. He would carry on a yoke — a frame of wood to go round the shoulders — two clean buckets with which to replace the dirty ones.

One day, while I was waiting for my grandmother to come out of the toilet, I was amazed to see her rush out with her knickers round her feet and run like a mad thing up the hill. When I caught up with her I saw she was shaking like a leaf and she told me why. It seemed that while she was sitting there she had heard a hissing sound and, moving only her eyes, had glanced up to see a snake getting ready to strike. No wonder she hadn't stopped to pull up her knickers!

Being the only house for many miles around, Grandmother was much sought after for her knowledge of first aid. One of the worst cases I remember was a workman, from a nearby quarry, who had been holding a stick of dynamite in his hand and wasn't quick enough in throwing it into the cavity of the pit. It blew out the palm of his hand. The white overseer had rushed him over to Grandmother who had stemmed the flow of blood, cleansed him as best she could and treated him for shock, until the ambulance arrived to take him to the mission hospital.

All our shopping, for fruit and vegetables, was done at the back door. The women of the village would bring them to the house in huge baskets, which they carried on their heads. To keep the basket from falling off their heads, Zulu women had adopted a very graceful, leisurely and relaxed way of walking which gave them a very proud look. They achieved this walk by placing their naked feet gently and firmly in a straight line, one in front of the other. When I was in a convent I was made to walk the same way, but with books on my head.

The women would squat down and place the baskets on the ground in order to display their wares. These goods were never bought with money but were bartered for trinkets (the flashier the better) and brilliantly coloured materials. Grandmother seemed to have an ever-flowing stream of these trinkets and materials, and I was allowed to play with them in the lovely sunshine, where they dazzled and sparkled with the beautiful colours emanating from them.

As our house was built so high up, the garden could be seen by all the liners on their way to England, and if any of our friends were passengers they would stand on deck facing us and I would wave until they were out of sight. In order to make things easier for them we would lie a very large white sheet or tablecloth on the lawn, which we were told later looked exactly like a mantle of snow.

The tea plantation itself ran along the side of the house and I often went down there to see the women and children as, singing all the while, they picked off the tender young shoots from the tea bushes. These are pruned to encourage growth and to keep them about three to five feet for easy picking.

The pickers either had bags or baskets hanging from their heads or shoulders, and only the buds and first two leaves were picked and tossed into their baskets. When they had picked enough, the tea was weighed before being taken to the racks, which were outside. It was then spread out and left for twenty-four hours to soften. The next step was to have the leaves rolled and twisted by a machine in order to extract the juice. They were now ready for fermentation, and were left in a low temperature in a darkened room, from which all sunlight had been excluded. Remaining there for five to six hours, they gradually turned a beautiful golden-brown and were then ready to go to a room which was very hot, where the air circulated over and through them until they were completely dry and unable to ferment further. Eventually they were ready for grading and being sorted into very small, medium and larger leaves, by a machine consisting of sieves with varying mesh.

After I had been walking, watching all the interesting things on the plantation, I would go home, put on my swimming costume and go down the garden path to the little gate and thence straight onto the beach, with its white sand with golden glints shining in the sunlight. I would go for a swim in the clear blue sea, which had 'sea horses' all along the top of the waves. That name was given to the white spume which made them look exactly like white horses tossing their heads and prancing in the sea.

If I was very lucky I'd be there when real horses were brought down to be cooled and washed, and I would be allowed to ride one of them through the water. It was a wonderful feeling when the waves lapped against the horse's side, right over its back and therefore all over me.

Although the beach sounds an idyllic place, it could suddenly become very frightening when sand storms blew up. I was only caught once and fortunately had an aunt with me (who was visiting at the time). She rushed out of the sea, dragging me with her, and burrowed on her side into the sand to act as a bulwark for me, as she pushed me down in front of her for protection from the swirling sand. When the storm had subsided (they stop as suddenly as they start), she stood up and her back was covered in minute spots of blood where the sand had hit her. Since growing up, I now realise how brave she was and how she stopped me from getting really hurt.

Not far from the house were leafy lanes which led down to a lagoon, not far from the beach. This particular one was really beautiful, with a rich profusion of trees and shrubs, that made a sanctuary for the lovely, twittering birds. Some colonies of birds had nests made of twigs which were huge. They hung down like a maze of netting. These were communal nests and were used by more than a hundred birds. Unfortunately snakes could climb into them and live off the eggs. This is, of course, one of nature's ways of keeping down the bird population, but the funny thing is that the snake doesn't eat them all, and when he leaves the nest he is very careful not to crack any of the eggs left behind.

The weaver bird, the swallow of Africa, is small and very often gaily coloured. Their nests always fascinated me because there were hundreds of them. They were woven together with twigs and grass with the top structured like a dome, which they entered from below through a long passage built onto the roomy dome. They always nested near people, especially near African villages.

I think my favourite bird, though, was the beautiful kingfisher, with its scintillating blues and greens, and long feathered crest. They are, of course, always found by water. When in its whirring, swift flight it looked exactly like a jewel, shining in the sun, with azure, turquoise, purple and peacock green, or the metallic green of the firefly. They lived in nests which they dug in the bank of the lagoon, looking like a tunnel with a round room at the back lined with fish bones, in which to lay their eggs.

I liked to watch the jacana, or lily trotter, with its long legs and talons which helped it to walk on any floating water-plant. Another odd little bird which is only to be found in Africa, was called the mouse bird, because of its ability to move its outer toes backwards and forwards, so it could climb and run among the trees like a mouse.

I was very lucky having a grandfather who took an interest in birds, and taught me to get to know them. Remember, he began life as a country boy. He told me the names of many of the local African birds, but there are too many for me to remember after all these years. I think you can realise why I loved the lagoon and spent as much time as possible there.

One day I went there for a picnic with my brother, and some cousins who had come from Durban to stay with us for a holiday, taking sandwiches and pop to drink, also coconut milk, which we all liked. After we had eaten, and thrown the crumbs to the birds, we started to sing, at first very quietly in order not to disturb the birds; but all of a sudden we started to sing, at the top of our voices, a popular song of 1922 called 'Maggie'. What a noise there was! We really frightened the poor birds. They must have thought we were in competition with them, as they flew all over the place making more noise than us!

I could only go there in the early morning or late afternoon, as after a lunch of fruit, bread and butter and a drink of milk, I would have to go and lie down on a mat on the floor of my bedroom. This was because it was 'siesta' time, and I would have to stay there until the midday sun had lost some of its heat. The only place you could feel any air circulating was on the floor — hence my reason for lying there! Feeling very refreshed on waking up, I would go to the ice cooler to get a drink of pure, cold water. These coolers looked exactly like the hot water cistern over the sink in a kitchen but this one held lots and lots of ice.

As I was too young to go to boarding school, I took my first lessons with my brother who was being taught by a tutor who lived in the house with us. Actually it was the tutor who gave me my first swimming lesson, when I was four years old, and within a few weeks I could swim like a fish (well, almost!)

Our very happy years at Doonside were coming to an end, and when it became time for us to leave and go to East London to live, I was most unhappy, even though Sixpence and his whole family were coming with us — apart from his eldest sons, who were working on the tea plantation. Mind you, once Sixpence started telling me what a grand place East London was, and how they were all looking forward to moving, I felt much better and ready to face going to a village school there.

Chapter 11

East London — sugar cane — school — snakes and things

As East London was approximately 800 miles from Doonside, you can imagine the kerfuffle caused by moving. The amazing thing was that the Zulus from the kraal, who were coming with us, walked the whole way. They kept in single file, carrying their 'bits and pieces' on their heads, with even the youngest toddler carrying a bundle.

Most of our luggage went by ox-wagon and we travelled in horse-driven wagons as far as Cape Town, when we transferred to a train to finish the journey to our new East London home. This, of course, took many days, but to our surprise, when we arrived at the bungalow on the edge of the beach, everything was already 'ship-shape', as Sixpence and his family had arrived there first! Even the mosquito-nets were around the beds. The bungalow was, of course, built up on the usual legs and again was light, spacious and airy. It also had an outside staircase which led onto a flat roof. I loved to sit or lie up there, especially on a warm, dark night, and gaze up at the twinkling stars which seemed to shed a ghostly brilliance over the brooding quietness of the surrounding area. By the way, I can never remember furniture being moved, so can only assume that the various places we lived in were already furnished.

East London was situated at the mouth of Buffalow River, where it met the sea. It was built in the times of the frontier wars as a harbour for the garrison town of King William, not far inland. First of all they named it Port Rex, nailing a Union Jack to a tree on Signal Hill, near the entrance to the harbour. Some years later a man called Harry Smith claimed the harbour as British and renamed it East London, and so it has remained ever since.

East London was a beautiful place, with lovely clear streams, enclosed on three sides by soft green country, with the deep blue sea in front. The sea was not always calm; it could become very savage and stormy. It had been known to cause an awful lot of damage, and sink many ships, with a freak wave described as a 'precipice of water', which made a great hole in the sea into which the ships had fallen, and then been engulfed. I was only taken to see it a couple of times, as we lived some miles away on one of the beautiful beaches in the suburbs. The beach was split up into three sections, one part set out for fishermen, one for swimmers, and the other for a children's paddling pool.

One day after school I had gone down for a swim, when I noticed that one of our neighbours, a keen fisherman, seemed to be dancing very energetically indeed, and I learnt later that he had actually been shocked by an electric eel which he'd caught. He was one of the lucky ones, as I heard that many men had been electrocuted when taking them off the hook.

I now attended the village school which was about two miles away, and used to walk with seven other children, armed with sticks in case we saw any snakes. The pathway to school went through a sugar plantation where we saw the labourers cutting the sugar canes with machetes (a very broad, one sharp-sided, flat knife). We were nearly always given a piece to suck, after it had been stripped of its bark, as there was a soft pithy centre left which was full of sugary juice. On arrival at school we would have to wash our sticky faces and hands again!

When walking through the plantation we had to keep strictly to the well-trodden path, because sugar cane grows to a height of 17ft-20ft, and one could easily get lost in it, also the men cutting it down wouldn't be able to see you and you could end up having your legs cut off!

I only saw one snake (a cobra) whilst in South Africa, and that was lying curled up asleep in the middle of one of the lanes I used to walk down. I remember rushing home to call out the house and field boys, who came tearing down with knobkerries in their hands. A knobkerrie is a very heavy piece of wood with a round head, which was usually used by Africans as a weapon. They proceeded to beat the poor thing to death, with the help of us children! When I think of it now my blood runs cold and I wonder how I could have possibly helped them to slaughter it in such a cruel way. I only hope there are now more humane ways of controlling them.

Amongst the five different species of the cobra family the most poisonous, dangerous and largest is the Black Mamba (an adult can measure anything from 7ft-11ft). They are extremely quick movers, can climb if they have to, but prefer to live on the ground.

A fascinating snake is the saw-scaled viper, as it has saw-like edges along the side of its body, and when it lies curled around in loops, they rub against each other causing a loud, bubbling, frothy sound.

Another very dangerous and frightening snake is the puff adder; when it is scared it hisses and inflates itself to twice its natural size (5ft long and it can be 9" thick). It's very poisonous and its bite nearly always proves fatal.

Our school was built of bricks, and had a tin roof. There were three school-rooms plus the headmaster's study and a room for the teacher. As there were only a dozen children attending the school the headmaster, who was a Scot, taught the older children while the lady teacher, also a Scot, taught the younger children, which included me.

On arriving at school one day I was sent back home, together with the other children, because our teacher hadn't arrived and we were told she was in hospital. It seemed that during the night a python had got through a hole in her bedroom floor, and she had woken up to find it slithering over her chest. She was frozen with fear but had kept completely still, which was the best thing she could have done. Eventually she noticed out of the corner of her eyes that it had slid out of her bedroom and down over the side of the veranda; it was then that she screamed and screamed, and didn't stop screaming until she was sedated and taken to hospital to get over the shock.

Another day, whilst walking home along the lane, I heard the most awful noise of a squawking chicken and to my horror saw it running towards me with its head off. Apparently the cook had cut it off, when it suddenly started to squawk, flapped its wings and took off! When eventually the cook caught it, he hung it up on the line until it had stopped flapping its wings, as he himself was afraid to hold it. I went indoors and cried bitterly but was assured that it was only the heat that had kept the chicken's nerves alive, and that it wasn't in pain at all. I accepted the explanation at the time but as I became older I was never 100% sure.

One of the highlights in my life occurred on 15th July 1921, my sixth birthday. I woke up very early, as Grandfather had told me the night before that he was arranging a very special birthday treat for me.

It was a beautiful morning and I decided to wear my best dress of blue and white checked gingham, with a dimity apron made of strong white cotton which covered the front and back of my dress. The apron was dropped over the head and tied each side with ribbons. The back was quite plain but the front had beautiful lacy ruffles which ran the full length of each side. I also wore white socks and black patent leather, ankle-strapped shoes. On my head I wore a sun-hat which was shaped like a poke-bonnet in front (that shaded the face) and had a length of puckered cotton material hanging from the crown of the hat to the shoulders, which shielded the nape of my neck from the hot sun.

Grandfather's treat was revealed when he told me that a chauffered car would be calling to drive us and Granny to see a business friend of his, who was a silk merchant and also an Indian prince. Eventually the car arrived and we were driven several miles to a beautiful bungalow which was set in lovely surroundings. One could see right through the wide open windows of the bungalow to a gloriously brilliant garden, with a view of fields, hills and picturesque highlands in the background.

We found the prince and his wife sitting in the shade of a pillared portico, when the car drove up to the entrance of the house. As we got out they stood up to greet us and escorted us into an extremely spacious and airy room. Young as I was I remember being very impressed, especially when I saw, suspended from the ceiling, two softly whirring fans which were almost hidden by a false ceiling of gently billowing silk of many shades of colour, that gave a cooling effect to the room.

We sat on piles of large beautifully coloured silk cushions, and I felt like a princess myself, sitting there drinking tea from very fragile cups without handles, which were decorated in pastel colours of pink and blue, etched out in gold leaf, and eating little cakes which were very, very sweet.

The prince himself was a tall, rather portly gentleman, with brilliant brown eyes. He wore a very white turban (the first one I'd ever seen), and was dressed in an ordinary morning suit, worn by most businessmen of this period. His wife was a most fascinating lady, slim and sinuous with almost coal-black eyes. Her dark hair was long, wavy and thick, and very shiny. She wore a pure white silk sari, dotted all over with pale pink pearls. If it wasn't for the lovely smile that lit up her whole face, she could have been a statue. I couldn't take my eyes off her.

After we had finished tea we were taken outside to see the prince's storehouse, in which were stored bales and bales of coloured silks ranging from pastel shades to the more exotic ones.

When it was time for us to go, after Grandfather had completed his business, the prince handed me a birthday present consisting of a lovely silk handkerchief, a blue butterfly brooch encased in silver and also an elephant's-hair ring, which was considered to be very lucky. What a wonderful end to the day and to a birthday which I have never forgotten.

Chapter 12

Train journey to Volksrust —
the farm — on holiday

We had been in East London for about two years when Grandfather decided we should have a holiday, and arranged to take us to a place called Volksrust, where his brother and sister-in-law lived. Oh! the hustle and bustle that went on to get ready for the train journey, which was to take four days. Such an assortment of luggage, from suitcases for day and night clothes, to basket hampers that contained tins of condensed milk and food of all descriptions, and of course a large one full of toys and books to keep everyone happy during the journey.

When a family was on the move they had their own railway carriage, thereby ensuring the family had plenty of room in which to move. If you arrived early at your destination, as we did, the carriage would be taken to a siding, unhooked and left there until your hosts came to collect you.

This particular journey proved to be a very exciting one, and also very interesting as, apart from getting caught up in a plague of locusts, we travelled through some very beautiful countryside. Starting from East London, in Cape Province, we were about to begin a journey of approximately 448 miles. Our first stop was at Umtata to 'water' our engine. Every couple of hundred miles you would see, standing by the side of the railway lines a few yards away from the station, tall, wide, erect pipes with arms at the top which held a long canvas sleeve. The canvas sleeve would be moved just over the top of the engine, where the tank opening was situated, and the water would be pumped straight into it.

Our second stop was Pietermaritzburg, where fresh fruit and

milk was bought from the vendors who squatted by the side of the railway lines. We were now in the province of Natal and had completed just over half of our journey.

The vast swarm of locusts we encountered near Ladysmith, bombarded our train like hailstones and hundreds were squashed on the rails before the driver was able to bring the train to a halt. It was very frightening indeed, as one moment we were in brilliant sunshine and all of a sudden it was as if someone had thrown a heavy black blanket completely over us, blotting out the outside world.

The female of these awful insects, which are a species of grasshopper, lays about seventy eggs or so which are bound together by a frothy substance she secretes from her body, which has been swollen to half the size of her body-weight. She lays them as far down in the sand as possible and they only emerge 10-14 days later if the temperature is approximately 95°. When they are first born they are known as 'hoppers', as they are wingless, and it is only after shedding several skins that their wings will appear, about forty days later, when the adult locusts swarm. They have been known to cover an area of 250 sq. miles. The unfortunate thing is that they eat everything in sight in a very short space of time. Where they have passed there is not a blade of grass, crop of mealies or green leaves to be seen. The countryside is stripped bare. Consequently, they do untold damage to the economy of S. Africa and they are very, very difficult to control.

When the driver was able to see daylight again, he had the lines and the wheels of the train hosed down so that we were able to continue our journey.

After leaving the locusts behind, we were then travelling through veld country, which is the high grass tableland country of the Transvaal, in South Africa. There are three levels of this plateau land: the low or bush veld, about 1000ft-3000ft; the middle veld about 2000ft higher; and the high veld, between 500ft and 600ft above sea level. It was a very beautiful grassy landscape through which we travelled, very open and completely unforested. The grass was lush and plentiful, making it extremely good grazing land, and you could see through the train window the contented looking cattle, busily munching and chewing the cud.

Grandfather devised many different games in order to keep us interested in all that was going on around us. One of these games consisted of seeing how many different animals we could spot, whilst looking out of the train window. Suddenly I saw hundreds of springbok bounding along, with a succession of jumps of about 8ft, landing as light as feathers.

One night, when I was unable to sleep, I pulled the curtains apart and looking out into the darkness, saw the moon rise. What a thrilling experience — she arrived in all her glory, flooding the veld with light and throwing a silver sheen over the wide expanse of dense forest in the distance. Here and there a river could be seen gliding on its silvery way, just like a snake. Nearer to the train was a vast terrain of rich, undulating grassland where, in the mysterious darkness, I could just discern herds of cattle.

Volksrust, on the Natal-Transvaal border (mealielands of the Transvaal's high veld) was a junction for trains, and when we arrived very early in the morning, our carriage was shunted into the sidings and left there while we finished our sleep. On awakening, and looking out of the windows, I was very excited to see that the earth and station were covered in white stuff, being informed that it was snow. I had never seen so beautiful a scene and thought I had woken up in fairyland.

In 1878 a group of people trailed by ox-wagon along the road from Durban and camped near the mountain top. This group consisted of the first Anglican bishop, the Right Rev. Henry, his wife and eight children. They had left Andover, England, to be missionaries, and at 7.00 am on Christmas morning he held his first communion there.

My cousin and his father came to collect us in a horse and carriage, and two of their farm boys had brought an ox-wagon for our luggage. We enjoyed a lovely breakfast of mealie-meal (maize) porridge, with its warm, frothy, fresh cow's milk and the spoonfuls of golden syrup, which my Aunty Jenny had ready for us; it tasted like nectar from the Gods!

After breakfast my fourteen year old cousin Alec took me to see his underground house, which he had dug himself. He had made a long corridor with two rooms each side. In each room he had scooped holes in the wall for chairs, and had left a flat-topped block of earth for a table; it was only high enough for children to stand up in, so no adults could enter. What a joy it was, taking our food and drink down there to have a picnic. It was also a veritable treasure-house, with most of my cousin's prized possessions being kept down there. I felt as if I was Alice in Wonderland, and expected to see the white rabbit down there with us!

The local market, about twenty minutes walk from the farm, was also something of an Aladdin's cave, with all the bead and basketwork, bronze and copper sculptures, bracelets, and baskets and baskets of fruit and coconuts. I remember my aunt buying forty pineapples, which had been hung on two poles; they cost 12½p and were carried home by the houseboys. The poles were balanced between them from shoulder to shoulder, and as the poles were so flexible, they swayed to the rhythm of their trotting and singing. As some of my aunt's maids had come as well, with empty baskets, they were able to carry the rest of the fruit, such as the mangoes and guavas — very luscious fruit with a lovely taste — and also the melons and pumpkins.

As we were in the Transvaal area Grandfather decided, as part of the holiday, that he would take me over the border into Southern Rhodesia, to see the mighty cascade of the Victoria Falls. Dr Livingstone discovered them in 1885, and was supposed to have said, "I saw a stream of a thousand yards broad which leaped down a hundred feet and was suddenly compressed into a space of fifteen to twenty yards." These were the falls of the great Zambezi River, which are higher and have a far greater expanse of water than the Niagara Falls, between Canada and the USA (twice as high and nearly twice as wide). 'The greatest river wonder of the world', is the way Lord Curson (British statesman and Viceroy of India, 1898-1905) described the falls.

They hurl the Zambezi River over the cliff edge at approximately 75,000,000 gallons a minute. The fall of the water sets up a drenching rain, as you walk through what is called the rain forest (which lies along the edge of the cliff for a mile, facing the falls) and also very strong winds, as the air being forced downwards can only escape by going upward from the bottom, forcing vapour from the falling waters into a pillar of cloud which rises about fifty feet into the air, and can be seen for many miles, with its iridescent colours of the rainbow, shining and gleaming through it.

Walking along the rain forest you can see another cliff, equally high up, with a gap 100ft wide and about a mile between them. This is a cavity into which the waterfall thunders. You carry on walking and pass the various parts of this great phenomenon, such as the Eastern Cataret, the Boiling Pot, Rainbow Falls, Livingston Island, Main Falls, Cataract Island and Devil's Cataract, all of them within a short distance of each other.

A statue of David Livingstone stands on the spot where he first saw the falls and named them after Queen Victoria; the natives call them Musi-Oa-Tunya (The Smoke That Thunders).

The Cape to Cairo railroad, with its high bridge, crosses over the gorge a little below the falls, then goes through the narrow strip of land that divides the bend of the returning rapids, from the corner of the plunging cataract. It runs so close to the falls that passengers can feel the spray from the descending water. It really is a wonderful sight and very, very impressive. I am so pleased I saw it.

Chapter 13

Kruger National Park, Johannesburg, and Pretoria

During our journey to Johannesburg we talked non-stop about our coming trip to Kruger National Park. It was one of the first game reserves in which wild animals roamed at will, and gamekeepers were employed to ensure public safety by seeing that they remained in their cars while driving through the park. They were also employed to see that the animals were well treated.

The route to the reserve ran through beautiful orange groves, and I remember being allowed to pick and eat one of the oranges. I have never forgotten my first glimpse of the great plains that rose in steps toward the majestic Drakensberg mountains, and the many rushing rivers that shone and sparkled under a clear blue sky.

You can imagine how nervous I felt when a herd of elephants began to cross the road on which we were travelling. We had to stop the car while two bulls and two cows (male and female elephants) together with their three calves trundled across. We noticed that every so often the adult elephants would pull a branch of a tree right off, in order to give their youngsters a meal. Because elephants are so large they tend to knock and trample down anything that gets in their way.

I particularly loved watching the monkeys, as they seemed so human, especially in the protective way they looked after their babies. My favourite, and the ones I liked feeding and talking to, were called Diana's. They were really pretty, with a white crescent (like a new moon) on their forehead and what looked like a white beard and a scarf round the neck.

Our day out at the park passed far too quickly for me, and I was really sorry when the time came for us to leave. On leaving the park I turned back to look at the mountains and asked my grandfather to stop the car for a few minutes. It was such a fantastic sight, as the sky was now bathed in the many coloured hues of sunset, and the evening stars and moon were just appearing in the heavens above. It was a sombre, weird and grand scene, as every valley, hill and tree shone with the pale cold lustre of moonlight.

The friends with whom we were staying only lived about three miles from the reserve, and they were very kind people. I felt a little nervous of the man, though. He seemed so tall and had a thin face with a hole above his temple, on which the skin throbbed so violently I kept thinking it would burst and I would see blood spurt all over the place. He must have sensed my fear, as he gently held my hand and told me that many years ago, on a very dark night, he was driving home and failed to see a boulder lying in the middle of the road. He was thrown out of the car onto his face and a sharp, pointed stone pierced his forehead. This had caused his disfigurement, therefore I had nothing to be frightened of. His wife was such a rosy-cheeked woman, round and fat like a dumpling, and always seemed to wear an old felt hat. Occasionally she would take me with her to see and help with the milking of the goats — ten in all. They were rather smelly but very useful animals, and were kept mainly for their milk.

When we first arrived at their bungalow from the park, I was really surprised and happy to see, on getting out of the car, that two monkeys were calmly sitting on top of the roof. They were chained up in the garden until one of the game wardens arrived to take them back.

Next morning saw us once again on the train, this time travelling a short distance (approximately 60 miles) to Johannesburg, the City of Gold, named after the surveyor-general, Johannes Rissik, whose name is perpetuated by Rissik Street where the city hall now stands; it was opened in 1915, the year of my birth!

There were three things that greatly impressed me about Johannesburg: the African museum which housed photographs, books, cuttings and relics depicting the early history and outstanding events that had made Johannesburg the great city of South Africa, and which was more or less built on golden earth! When gold was first discovered, President Pretorius wasn't interested as he was far more concerned with the welfare of his Boer farmers and their land. He refused to issue licences to diggers because he was worried that amongst the genuine mining engineers and their families, would come 'riff-raff' from all corners of the globe. Eventually though, big business won and gold seekers from all over the world arrived. Unfortunately Pretorius was proved right, as many tramps, vagabonds, loose women and rogues were to be found amongst the new prospectors of gold.

Because of the growth of the mining of gold, a small school of mining and technology was opened in 1903; but it progressed to such an extent, that by 1921 it had incorporated schools of medicine, art, and architecture, while still retaining its mining interests, and as such had officially become the University of Witwatersrand.

I didn't care very much for the post office, which had been built in 1887, because I thought it very ugly. It was very gaudy, in red and pale green, with a towering clock-tower (106ft) which stands straight opposite the very beautiful city hall.

The last place I was taken to see were the Sterkfontein Caves, where so much gold-digging had gone on in the early prospecting days. They found a skull of a child down there which had been preserved by the lime-encrusted rocks; it turned out to be almost a million years old. They called it the Tuang Baby. Twelve years later another ape-man was found, this time an adult. Since then hundreds of bones and skulls have been found, which proved there had been a tribe living in that area.

A guide led us down into the very bowels of the earth, holding a lantern which threw very eerie shadows among the many stalagmites and stalagtites, and pools of light that glowed amongst the rocks! My imagination was working overtime, as I began to feel as if the ape-men were hiding in the dark and watching me. I was really glad to get back into daylight.

We only stayed in Johannesburg three days, as Grandfather wanted me to finish this educational holiday in Pretoria, prior to travelling 448 miles back to East London.

Leaving Johannesburg was no hardship to me, for although I had thoroughly enjoyed my visit, I didn't really like all the hustle, bustle and noise of the crowded streets.

The contrast between Johannesburg, the City of Gold, and Pretoria, the capital of the Transvaal, has to be seen to be believed. Pretoria nestles on the lower veld at the base of the Magaliesberg range of mountains, in a truly sylvan setting of valleys, streams, grassy plains and beautiful trees; whereas Johannesburg was, to my eyes, rather a dreary, dusty town, built on the high bare veld (almost 6,000ft above sea level) with its man-made hills consisting of tons of machinery-crushed rock, that was left over by the old prospectors delving down to the netherworld for gold!

In 1840 a small group of trekkers entered the valley of the Apies River with their families. They saw the lovely Fountains Valley, which was deserted except for the myriads of little monkeys who lived in the trees and who gave the river its name of Apies — Monkeys' — River.

The trekkers camped under the trees, were married and had their children christened beneath their shade. It was from these small beginnings that Pretoria developed. In 1854 the trekkers built the first Dutch Reformed Church, and by 1860 the village which had grown up around it became the seat of the government of South Africa. Fifty years later, in 1910, it became the administrative capital of the Transvaal.

All my life I have loved trees of all kinds, and I think this love affair actually started with my stay in Pretoria. I thought it one of the loveliest places I have ever seen, with its wide, jacaranda-lined streets. These trees are not native to South Africa but were first introduced into the country by an American, who grew them in his garden, having brought them from tropical South America in 1889. His trees are the parents of Pretoria's beautifully shady jacarandas, with their lovely blooms of violet-mauve bells. They grow in such great profusion all over the town that it is often referred to as Jacaranda City. One of the loveliest sights is obtained by walking to the summit of one of the hills and gazing down onto the shimmering mauve haze of the blooms, which seem to cover all the steep flowery streets in the valley below.

One of the first places I was taken to see was Paul Kruger's old home, which was built for him in 1884 in very simple flowing lines, long, low and with a veranda running its entire length in front, on which the president would sit to discuss affairs of state, whilst drinking coffee with his colleagues. It is now a museum and the inside of the house has been restored as near as possible to the original old style in which the Krugers lived.

The Transvaal museum is also very interesting and very eye-catching, with the skeleton of a large-fin whale standing in front of it. Inside is a collection of hundreds of South African birds which was put together by an amateur ornithologist, Austen Roberts, in 1910. By his writings he became one of the first authors to educate his readers to take an interest in bird life.

The next interesting historical building, was the place where Winston Churchill had been imprisoned after his capture by the Boers in 1899. He was a war correspondent for the London *Morning Post* and was taken prisoner near Estcourt in Natal and brought to Pretoria. He was only there a month before he managed to escape on December 12, 1899 by climbing over a tall iron fence and hiding in the bush on the banks of the Apies River.

One of Pretoria's famous houses is Melrose House which was built in 1886 as a home for a merchant, George Heys, and from which he ran a coaching service, 'Express Saloon Coaches', during Kruger's days, and which carried the mail for many years. Melrose House is a great big Victorian mansion, all plush, with mirrors, and very heavy looking; some people consider it a monstrosity, and others magnificent! It has turrets, a large conservatory, stained-glass windows, and an organ which was transported from America. The builder was a London architect who had English materials shipped over; it was conveyed over land to the site by ox-wagon.

The end of my holiday was now in sight and I was quite ready for the long slow train journey home, although I was a little apprehensive about the questions I knew my grandfather would be asking me about which, what or who had made the greatest impression on me and why? He was determined to keep my mind active at all costs, and perhaps it was just as well because I wouldn't have been able to remember enough to get even this story started!

Chapter 14

Journey to Cape Town — Newlands

We had been in East London for about six months after our holiday, when Grandfather said we were to go and stay in a hotel in Cape Town, and as Sixpence and his family would not be able to come this time, they decided to go back to their old kraal in Doonside.

I was very sad, knowing that this was probably the last time I would ever see them, but I knew in my heart that I would always remember them with deep affection and very fond memories.

I was quite happy to be on the move again, as I had so enjoyed travelling around on our holiday and wanted to see more. Once again it was to be a long train journey, as Cape Town was over 500 miles from East London, and this time we would be travelling in the opposite direction.

Port Elizabeth was our first stop, to 'water' the train and buy fresh fruit and provisions. It had rather a small harbour, which was used mainly for small boats belonging to the fishermen.

We had several hours to spend there and were able to walk about, noticing that Port Elizabeth was a city of steep hills and narrow streets, also that it was a very windy place. Climbing up one of the hills I stood on the Donkin Reserve, a big open grassy area on the slopes, and looking down I could see the harbour, which looked smaller than ever, with its wood and iron jetties. Tugs were also anchored there, ready to carry passengers out to the liners lying some distance away from the harbour.

On this green grassy spot was a stone pyramid which had

been built in memory of Sir Rufane Donkin's young wife Elizabeth, who had died in India in 1818 at the age of twenty-seven. He was still mourning her death two years later, when he became acting governor of Cape Town and had this memorial erected, with the following inscription: *To the memory of one of the most perfect of human beings, who gave her name to the town below.*

Getting back on the train we travelled as far as Oudtshoorn, where we were transferred to a horse-drawn bus to the lovely little town of George (named after George III), then back onto a train to Stellenbosch, a suburb of Cape Town, in which the hotel we were to stay at was situated. It is the second oldest town in South Africa, Cape Town being the first. It was a lovely fertile green valley, with huge blue mountains in the background and many small brooks running in the gutters. Somehow or other most people talked about 'our beautiful village', with its whitewashed houses and hundreds of oak trees. I used to watch small boys filling baskets and sacks with acorns and selling them to the farmers, who fed them to their pigs. Needless to say, being a girl I wasn't allowed to join them, but had to keep clean in my gingham dress, frilly white apron, and poke-bonnet.

The main street was at one time a wagon road to Cape Town. I don't remember the name of the hotel in which we stayed, but I know people were always talking about it, because it was almost a hundred years old. They had an old slave bell there, which hung inbetween two strong, thick, white columns; it was rung whenever the slaves were wanted, and they had to come running in from the fields as fast as possible.

Stellenbosch had many vineyards, which looked very cool and shady. The first vines were taken there in the 1600s from Germany, wrapped in damp soil and sail-cloth. The first vines which were planted all died, but the second lot flourished and Stellenbosch became known as the heart of wine land. At the entrance to the Oude Meester Stellenryck Wine Museum was a massive wooden wine-press which had been made in 1790.

Stellenbosch also boasted a university at which Field-Marshal Jan Christian Smuts was educated. He was a very daring and formidable enemy of the British during the Boer War, and later became Prime Minister of the Union of South

Africa and a staunch friend of England.

Cape Town itself was a wonderful place, with Devil's Peak to the left of Table Mountain, and Signal Hill and Lion's Head to the right. I often walked along the boulevard which led toward the harbour docks, with its strong smell of the sea, and its historical background. I also visited the castle which was built in the seventeenth century; it looked more like a fortress from Europe, than anything African. It was built of stone, with cannons standing on the top of the bastions. The moat which surrounded it had a drawbridge, which was its only link with the outside world. Although it was very impressive it didn't look right, set in the shade of the mountain.

On the far left of the courtyard it had a balcony which everyone admired, and from which, in the 1800s, proclamations had been read. It was a most beautiful piece of wrought-ironwork balustrades, heraldic carvings and panelled doors.

Just outside the large pillared building of the South African Library stood a huge statue of Cecil Rhodes, but the first statue erected in the country was one to the memory of Shakespeare.

As we had to stay in the hotel for several months, whilst Grandfather looked around for a house for us to live in, I had to attend school. This was The Cape Town High, which was about a mile away. Apart from English I had to learn Boer's Dutch, which was the official language, and an educational law.

I thoroughly enjoyed going there, especially as I seemed to be lucky in my friends and teachers. I lost one of my friends though, through the headmaster coming into our classroom one day and asking us a mental poser. This particular friend of mine was — at least so I thought — a very clever girl, and when she came up with two answers, she asked me to say one of them. I agreed, possibly because I hadn't a clue what he was talking about and hadn't even attempted to work it out. After a few minutes he told us to stand up and walk toward him in single file to whisper the answer in his ear. Just before we reached him, my friend changed her mind and asked me to give the other answer, which I did. The headmaster asked me to remain near him for a few moments and when all the other children were back in their places and sitting down, he asked me my name; he then told me to go back to my place.

Later that day, he assembled the schoolchildren in the main hall, called me out and told them I was the only one amongst them all to have given the correct answer! He then proceeded to ask me to explain to them all how I'd arrived at the answer. I was petrified, so hung my head and kept my hands behind my back. He thought I was shy, so helped me out by saying, had I done so-and-so and so-and-so? All I could do was nod my head and to crown it all I received a prize of a gold watch. As I wouldn't give it to my friend, she didn't speak to me again. I don't blame her, do you?

The school itself was a large, brick-built building, just like the early schools of England, as Cape Town was a civilised place with all mod. cons, but not quite as modern as it is today. It was only two-storied, with five classrooms and a library and gym downstairs; upstairs contained the head-master's study, which overlooked the play area so he could see at all times exactly what was going on. Lessons started at 7.30 am as it was always 'siesta' time in the afternoons.

There was always a fully trained nurse in attendance at the hotel, which was a very good thing. One afternoon I went outside with my brother and some other children who were staying there. We were, of course, in bare feet; it was quite the accepted thing to do out there in those days, but it was absolutely forbidden for us to go outside the hotel grounds. Needless to say, we decided to take a walk down the road, and suddenly came across a man-hole. One of the boys removed its cover and we were all clustered around it, peering into its murky depths, when suddenly the boy slammed it down and my poor brother's toe was in the way. About a quarter of the toe disappeared down the hole! All at once, all hell was let loose, as my brother sat on the floor holding his toe, going round in circles on his bottom and screaming at the top of his voice.

The nurse came running, rushed him indoors and sent for the doctor. He was there in a very few minutes, anaesthetized my brother and took off the top joint of his toe. He did this to make sure none of the filth from the cover was lurking inside, and to make sure he didn't catch tetanus.

Grandmother was absolutely shattered to hear about it when she arrived back from the dentist, where she'd had troubles of her own having a gum-boil lanced through the side of her jaw-bone. Poor soul, she was really ill next day, while my brother suffered no ill-effects and was soon up and about again.

One very unusual event occurred. One afternoon there were blood-curdling yells coming from a group of horsemen who, dressed in flowing burnous (a mantle with a hood) and whirling swords above their heads, were riding at full gallop along the road. All the people staying at the hotel were rushed inside from the garden, and all doors and windows were barred. It seems there were often small skirmishes or uprisings going on, so the hotel staff knew exactly what to do.

Amongst the many ladies staying there was one who had bought a fur necklet and had worn it home round her neck. When she arrived back at the hotel she placed it on the bed in her room while she went into the bathroom to wash her face and hands, prior to going down for afternoon tea. When she went back she found it on the floor, picked it up and draped it over the back of a chair.

She had her tea and an hour's gossip then went back upstairs, and lo and behold, it was on the floor again. She picked it up and placed it in the middle of her double bed. Going over to the dressing table, she sat down and began brushing her hair. She happened to glance through the mirror at her fur and was horrified to see it wriggling about all over the bed. She flew to the door and shrieked at the top of her voice. One of the porters happened to be near and rushed in to see what the rumpus was. By this time the corridor was thronged with guests also anxious to know what was going on.

The porter realised at once that a snake had somehow been sewn into the lining of her fur, and that her body heat and movements had woken it up. I heard later that she swore never to wear a fur again, especially round her neck!

Grandfather had now found a bungalow for us in a beautiful suburb of Cape Town called Newlands. This was the first time we were to live in the countryside and away from the beach. Our new home was a very pretty one with a lovely garden, and it was very near a wide expanse of open country at the foot of Table Mountain, on which stood a huge statue of Cecil Rhodes. Why a memorial to an Englishman? Well, it was to commemorate his making South Africa part of the British Empire. He also planned to build the Cape-to-Cairo railway to the Cape of Good Hope, and the mouth of the Nile.

He was born on the 5th July 1853 at Bishop's Stortford, Hertfordshire. He was only twenty-eight years old when elected to the parliament of Cape Colony and nine years later became its Prime Minister, and virtually the dictator of South Africa. He also had vast business interests in diamond and gold mining and became managing director of the British African Company. One of the most impressive incidents in his career was during the revolt of Matabele natives in Southern Rhodesia. All attempts by the army to repress the rebellion failed, so Rhodes moved away from the troops and pitched his tent at the foot of the Matopo Hills (to where the natives had retreated) and patiently waited to see what would happen. The warriors were so amazed at his courage that they invited him to a council meeting. Before attending the council meeting, he rode back to the troop encampment to ask three of his friends to accompany him. They agreed and rode unarmed into the midst of the warriors. He listened to their grievances and promised to do something for them, so the uprising was over. Unfortunately he died on the 26th March 1902, broken in health from the seige which took place at Kimberley during the Boer War.

Two events stand out in my mind with regard to Newlands; the first was the parade of peacocks and peahens, about fifty of them, that seemed to cross the road at about 6.00 am every morning, waking everyone up with their raucous, unearthly screams. But what a picture they made with the drab-coloured hens amongst the males, with their fantastic plumage spread out like fans. The colours were so beautiful and brilliant: bronze, blue, green and gold.

The second event could have ended with dire consequences, but thankfully I'm still here to write about it. I used to walk about three miles to school, with eight other children, through a very leafy, shady country lane. About half-way along the lane we had to pass a general store which had six wooden steps leading up to the door. The smell of spices, herbs and tea assailed your nostrils as soon as you entered the shop; it was wonderful just to stand still savouring it all. We used to spend so much time in there that it was a wonder that we ever got to school at all!

I remember seeing bottles and bottles of black and red bulls'-eyes, and liquorice sticks, together with small sugared pin-cushions in many pastel shades. It used to be so difficult making up one's mind what to buy. My favourites though were the roasted burnt almonds and pine kernels from out of the pine-cones.

Close to the counter stood a small table with a tray full of small cheap books, with pictures on the covers and red, blue and yellow bindings. This is where I stood the longest, wondering which one I'd enjoy reading the most. I was very, very much of a bookworm as a child; my grandmother was always saying, "For goodness' sake take your nose out of that book!"

One day when we had walked about half-way to the shop, we noticed some men taking a few young bulls to the slaughter-house. Suddenly one of the animals broke loose and started to chase us. We ran and ran and managed to scramble into the shop and get behind the counter just before the bull broke through the door, scattering the books all over the place. We were very frightened and exhausted after all that running.

Fortunately a couple of the men quickly arrived on the scene and managed to control the animal, before it had done too much damage. The wooden steps though had to be removed, as they had been well and truly broken by the heavy weight of the bull.

The school I attended was quite small and only had about fifty pupils. The headmaster was of average height, broad, neat and clean-shaven, with very ruddy cheeks and black hair, and he always wore a monocle in his left eye. He always insisted that two lists of names were hung in the main hall on a Monday morning. One list contained the names of those children who had been naughty the previous week, and the other list the names of the good children. The naughty ones used to be split up and made to sit with the good children. This idea seemed to work, because as the term progressed, the naughty list always seemed to get shorter and shorter.

Learning geography used to be great fun, as we would each be given the name of a town such as Cape Town or Johannesburg, then we would have to draw a map of South Africa and the name you had been given was entered on it in the correct position. Then came the hard work, as we had to find out the history and natural products of the town shown and then write about it on our maps. The best map was always pinned up on the blackboard. I'm afraid mine never made that 'honoured' place, as I was never quick enough to finish my account in the stipulated time.

Living in Newlands, we were overshadowed by Table Mountain, so-called because it was flat on top and when the clouds covered it they looked exactly like a tablecloth. The first time I walked up it with my grandmother, we seemed to be the only ones going up; all the other people were hurrying down. It wasn't until we were about half-way up that we were stopped by the police, who told us that a young woman had been murdered and that they were looking for her murderer. So we had no option but to go down again.

A few weeks later I went with my brothers and grandfather, and this time made it to the top. Looking down you could see the shore of Table Bay. It was a fantastic experience; and Cape Town nestled right in the middle, at the foot of the mountain. The Atlantic coast, with a splendid buttress called the Twelve Apostles, lay to the west. It took us about three hours to walk, but the view was well worthwhile.

Botanists from all over the world go to the top of Table Mountain because of the hundreds of plants and flowers which abound there. It is also a paradise for bird watchers, especially for those who admire the Cape Sugar Bird, with its lovely long tail that streams in the wind; orange-breasted sunbirds, the red wing starlings and lots more.

One of the very vivid memories I have of Cape Town, was when the Naval regatta week was on. The public were invited to go on board for a day's visit, and to get on board, a canvas shute had been suspended between Duncan's Rock and the deck of the ship. Even the mums and dads seemed to enjoy it, though some of the older folk were taken out by a small pilot boat. It was a lovely feeling, whizzing down so far, and to know it was over the sea.

Once on board, one of the sailors would be detailed to look after you for the day. My escort gave me a guided tour of the ship, explaining the functions of the various bits of machinery, and also what all the different dials were for. When that was over, we had a lovely lunch and then joined in all the games and competitions which had been organised and for which we received prizes. To get back to the shore, a small naval vessel stood by to take us to the landing stage. In the evening, all the Navy gun-boats gave the most wonderful searchlight display I have ever seen. It was truly beautiful, with all the lights criss-crossing the deep velvety darkness of an African night.

About three miles from Cape Town is Groote Schuur which, because of its historical background, I had to see. It was once the home of Cecil Rhodes and is a very large estate. He eventually bequeathed it to the premiers of the United South Africa, for them to live in. It was built in the old Dutch style, surrounded by the most beautiful flower gardens imaginable; and of course, there was his huge statue overlooking the bay. What a pity we ever had to leave such a lovely place as Newlands, but our next stop had to be Durban.

Chapter 15

Kimberley — Bloemfontein

On our travels once more, and what a journey — almost 900 miles! Our first stop was Kimberley. We stayed there for two days, mainly to see the 'big hole', which is a must for all visitors as it was the first diamond mine to be worked. A platform had been erected around it for people to see how, from a circumference of almost a mile, its walls tapered down to a depth of about ninety feet in places. At the bottom was a pool of dark, dank looking water, which made you think of a bottomless pit.

Kimberley is of course called 'The Diamond City'. The people who live there are extremely friendly and only too anxious to talk and tell you stories of the old days, and how the first diamond was found. I believe there are many versions, but the one I was told concerned some children in 1866, who were seen by a farmer playing with some very pretty stones. He admired them so much that he asked their mother if he could take them with him to Kimberley (this took place on their farm, on the outskirts). He showed them to a dealer, who confirmed his suspicions that they were indeed diamonds. The dealer bought them and the farmer being an honest man, shared the proceeds with the mother of the children.

A couple of years later this same farmer, Schalk Van Niekerk, heard that a witch-doctor was wearing a very large and beautiful charm. He made sure he had some cattle with him when he went to see the doctor, as he intended to buy it. The Zulu was delighted and handed it over. It was found to be an 83½ carat diamond. Later, Schalk Van Niekerk sold it for £11,000 and it was named The Star of South Africa.

It wasn't long before the 'bush telegraph' had done its job only too well, and 'diggers' from all over the world started to arrive — by ox-wagon, riding, or walking from many miles away. They first of all started looking all along the Vaal River, and some of them actually found a few; the ones who were lucky went further afield, and found many more. The men now started flocking to the 'dry digs' as they were called, being a little inland from the river. At first the diggers thought they were just dried-up tracks, where the diamonds had been deposited by the rivers or floods, but it was noticed that the ground where most of the diamonds were found was circular, with first a red layer of soil and then a yellow one of clay, and further down was a section of blue. From this circular piece of ground came the famous diamond fields.

When it was realised that it was too difficult for individuals to mine them, the financiers stepped in, such as Cecil Rhodes, Alfred Beit, and Barney Barnato, as they could buy the machinery needed to dig deep.

At one time there were four main mines, but gradually they combined to become the renowned De Beers Consolidated Mines Ltd., who became the leading diamond suppliers in the world.

De Beer started his life in a very humble cottage, before he knew anything about diamonds. He first became involved because he owned some very rich ground and the syndicate bought the use of his name and his ground. His first office is now a museum-piece, and the first thing I noticed was how dark and heavily Victorian it was, with all the old records and photographs — all very interesting to look at, but as an eight year old I found it a bit dull! So I went outside, where I saw an old 22ft-long wagon with iron axles, which had actually been used in the diamond fields in the old days. This wagon, I was told, was made from 'stink wood' (I hid my face and blushed as I thought this was rude). Actually it was wood which came from some very evil-smelling trees of South Africa, which is very light and strong.

The wagon itself was called 'half-tented', which meant that only the back half was covered. Here all the bedding and the necessities required for a journey were packed, in order to keep them dry. There were also racks which held rifles, ammunition and the medical kit. It used to be pulled by sixteen oxen, but now it was kept as a relic of the past and I could just imagine myself travelling over the veld in it. The man, who let me sit in the driver's seat, was very nice. He had ginger hair, lots of freckles and lovely twinkling eyes, which gave him such a merry face; but the things I remember most about him were his very long arms! He told me it was due to driving the sixteen oxen in the old days, and that they had pulled so hard that they had actually been stretched. I never knew whether to believe him or not!

It was the museum and 'The Big Hole' — the first diamond mine of the town of Kimberley — that dominated the area. The museum was a miniature town of Kimberley and had all the bars and dance halls, just as they were in the early 1800s. It was very popular with the many visitors, who flocked to see how the 'diggers' lived in those days.

The boundaries of the first mine were not very clearly defined, and when the Boer's President Pretorius went to stake his claim, he did so by saying that it was on Transvaal land; but the diggers asked the British to take over. Britain at the time had no interest, so it was left to the diggers to set up their own establishment, and they even went so far as to electing their own president. Eventually Britain sat up and began to take notice and liking what they saw, decided they were interested after all and paid compensation to the Boers, to enable the diamond mines to become British.

Another historical landmark was the Kimberley market square, where the food was distributed to the people during the four month seige in the Boer War. A large gun called 'Long Cecil', which was used to defend the village, stood in front of the monument which commemorated those who had died.

On now to Bloemfontein (Fountain of Flowers). When the separate states of South Africa became a union in 1910, Bloemfontein became the judicial capital, and was the seat of the South African appeal court. This is why we were here, as Grandfather was appealing over the verdict of a court case he had had in Cape Town. (It seems that he had sold his shops to a combine who had paid him a deposit and promptly gone into liquidation.) Grandfather wasn't too happy over the outcome, hence Bloemfontein and the appeal court!

Only a few voortrekkers had settled in this area in 1840, but within a few years, the British government became interested in the new lands and sent in a British resident. Major Henry Douglas Warden bought the site of Bloemfontein for just £37/10. In 1845 it was handed back to the Boers and it became the capital of a new republic — the Orange Free State.

Gradually it became a place of importance. Kruger and Milne held their historic meeting in a small, one-roomed house, with a thatched roof and a floor smoothed over with cow dung, to work out the constitution of the New Union. That little house had been built by Major Warden, and during its one hundred years had been a church, school, town hall, museum and Parliament House.

Just above Naval Hill, so called because a British Naval Brigade had occupied it during the Boer War, men of the Wiltshire Regiment had picked out the outlines of a horse in whitewashed rocks. The area was now a small game reserve of animals which were so tame that they came to eat out of your hand.

Moving to the other end of the city, I actually started to cry when I saw the wonderful memorial to the 26,000 women and children who died in concentration camps, set up during the Boer War, by the British government. The Boers never forgot this and considered it one of the worst atrocities of the war! At the base of a very large, tall column is a woman with her dying child. A younger woman gazes into the distance. They looked so unhappy and so real; although the figures were all in a beautiful smooth bronze.

This was the last of our visits before going to live in Durban for a couple of years, prior to our journey home to England.

Chapter 16

Durban

Durban was a settled city by 1824, but at one time it was an isolated settlement hemmed in by hostile tribes. The town is situated on a land-locked bay on the coast of the province of Natal. It was an important commercial and residential centre, and widely known as a beautiful seaside resort, cascading over with colour from the lovely hibiscus and oleander with its lance-shaped leaves and red or white blooms. Natal's tropical climate, together with its glorious botanical garden, where oranges, bananas and various tropical fruit grew in abundance, made it a very popular holiday town.

The city backed onto a low green, well wooded hill, overlooking the deep blue bay with its miles of golden sands glistening in the sunshine. Along the promenade were rickshaws pulled by Zulu boys, wearing fantastic head-dresses of feathers and usually adorned with a remarkable crown of ox horns, which was a version of the old uniform of Zulu warriors. Sitting in a rickshaw and being taken for a ride along the sea-front, was an unforgettable experience. I noticed that the man pulling the rickshaw seemed to be floating in the air as his feet hardly touched the ground at all. He ran with a series of leaps and bounds, covering an amazing amount of ground in a very short space of time.

I noticed from the rickshaw, many indians plying their wares, also snake-charmers and magicians. It was a most comfortable feeling and I was sorry when my ride came to an end. Later I watched one of the magicians performing the 'Indian rope trick'. The Indian simply threw a piece of rope into the air where it became so rigid that a little Indian boy was able to scale up it as he would a tree. When the boy reached the top he completely vanished! The Indian magician then twirled a very sharp sword above his head and over the top of the rope, and I heard blood-curdling screams coming from the little boy, then saw drops of blood falling down onto the ground. You could have heard a pin drop, until the little boy, with a big grin on his face, slid down the rope again. When he reached the ground the rope immediately tumbled down and went completely limp.

Not far from the town's gardens was a memorial stone commemorating the fact that Winston Churchill had made the first speech of his career in December 1899 on that spot. This was after his escape from the Boers in Pretoria. When he sailed into Durban he was fêted and fussed over, as everyone considered him a hero.

The Old Museum was one of the first houses to have an encircling veranda, and was built in the 1770s. It was made from mangrove poles, tropical trees, twigs, was very coarsely painted, and it was also thatched. Inside, the furniture was actually heirlooms which the settlers had used. It was so interesting and so nice that I often went to look over it, and once I was even allowed to sit on one of the hard wooden seats.

Durban had a very large community of Indians. It seems that in the 1840s, hundreds of men had been taken from India, with about forty to fifty women to every one hundred men, to help with the cultivation of sugar. When the terms of their contracts had expired, they were given the option of either going back to India or staying on. Many of them decided to accept a piece of land in lieu of their passage money, and most of them became very prosperous traders and market gardeners.

One area just outside Durban, within walking distance, used to belong to the elephants. One story, told me by one of the old residents, who was eighty-seven years old and had been one of the old prospectors (he had decided in his sixties to settle down in Durban), was how one of the elephants chased the first mayor of Durban, George Cato. Fortunately he proved to be fleet of foot and managed to get out of its way. The elephants had been gone a long time before I went there, but what a lovely place it was with its big trees, and gardens full of the beautiful bougainvillaea, with their rosy or purple flowers. The birds were exquisite, such as the purple-crested lourie, with its violet, green and crimson colouring, and also the purple-banded sunbird.

Some of my happiest moments were spent sitting near the harbour, which was shaped like a scoop and was divided into various sections to accommodate anything from small fishing boats to the large passenger liners. Once I was allowed a trip in one of the tugs that towed four flat-bottomed cargo boats out to the liners, to be laden with the passengers' luggage and await collection on the quayside.

Many of the interesting stories of Durban were told to me by the old fishermen. They said how hard their lives had been in the 1800s, and how they had caught many a shark in the vicinity. That was why safety-nets were used in the marked out swimming area. You still had to be very careful when swimming, and just before we arrived in Durban a shark had been washed over the safety-net during a storm, although I don't think anyone was eaten!

They also suggested I asked my grandfather to take me to see the replica of the old sugar mill, which was the start of Natal's sugar industry. This mill was a memorial to one Edmund Moorwood, who had collected sugar plants in America and had decided that the tropical weather of South Africa would be the perfect place for them to grow. He made his first sugar press from the spar of a wrecked ship. This was turned by handles by several of his Zulu assistants, which made the juice run down many channels straight into a large cooking pot. He then added some lime and boiled it until it crystallized into sugar. When leaving the mill I was given a small lump of the old type sugar, which had turned into a hard, brown-coloured shiny crystal which looked rather like a jewel.

While we were in Durban, Grandfather developed malaria (which is an African fever caused by the tsetse fly). I happened to be playing on the floor in his bedroom when he suddenly started to shiver and shake and kept saying, "Fetch your grandmother, fetch your grandmother." I thought he was playing and started laughing and begging him to do it again. Suddenly my grandmother rushed in, covered him in lots of blankets and gave him a dose of something, which I found out later was quinine.

The doctor advised him to go to England to recuperate, so he made arrangements for me to stay at the Stella Maris Convent as a boarder, whilst he and Grandmother went away for a few months. This meant us leaving our home at Stamford Hill, which was at the foot of Beria Ridge. This ridge was a narrow one of red sand, extending roughly from north to south, rising steeply on both sides to a height of 500ft above sea level, and through it four different rivers had made narrow gaps.

As a special treat, before they left for England they took me to the bioscope (cinema) to see Charlie Chaplin and Jackie Coogan in *The Gold Rush*. Inside the bioscope were tables and chairs scattered all round the room, and the walls were covered in mirrors so that it didn't matter where you sat or looked, you didn't miss any of the picture. You didn't pay to see the film, but you had to have tickets for tea and cakes. The clatter of crockery and cutlery didn't matter, as in those days they were silent films.

Before we had to leave our house I had been attending Sunday school, which was held in a beautiful garden with long trellised archways, simply covered in vines with large clusters of juicy black grapes. If we had been especially attentive and could answer questions put to us on the Bible story we had been listening to, we would be allowed to pick a handful of those lovely grapes. Needless to say we were all very quick with our replies.

Well the day dawned when my grandparents had to take me to the convent, which was surrounded by high walls and large wrought-iron gates. We walked through them, with me lagging behind, into a courtyard with mango trees, which led into a very lovely garden in front of the convent itself. Mother Superior was there to greet us and ushered us into her room, which seemed to me to be very big, grim and forbidding after all the open, airy bungalows and houses I had lived in. After a cup of tea my grandparents kissed me and said their goodbyes.

My first night in a dormitory of twenty girls (ten beds each side) was spent crying bitterly as I was so frightened and unhappy. It was the first time that my life had been seriously disrupted since my father had died. Gradually I began to settle and accept it, and to show an interest in everything to do with boarding school.

As far as I remember our uniform consisted of a brown calico dress with Peter Pan collar. The usual plain dimity apron, white socks and patent leather, ankle-strapped shoes were worn, topped by a panama hat with a broad ribbon round the brim, which also hung down the back.

The first bell rang at 6.00 am when the business of getting up went on at full speed. We had to make our own beds (I'd never had to do it before) before washing, dressing and doing our hair ready for breakfast, when the next bell rang three quarters of an hour later.

An hour later we had to attend assembly in the main hall of the convent, to listen to Mother Superior giving us the dos and don'ts for the day. We were to cleanse our minds of all sinful thoughts, be gentle and courteous at all times, and to say our prayers regularly; all this whilst standing with our arms bent behind our backs and a long pole thrust through the crook in order to make us stand up straight and to stop us bending forward.

At about half past eight we were led from assembly by the teaching nuns to our classrooms which were across the other side of the courtyard. The school was a two storey brick building, and had long corridors with small windows built high up, in order to stop us day-dreaming by looking at the sky or gardens. All the way to the school you could hear the nuns saying, "Tread lightly, young ladies. You should not make a sound when walking, just glide along!"

Apart from sewing and art we had the same nun for all subjects. It was thought to make for continuity of lessons. We had to work until 10.30 am, when we had a twenty minute break for a milk drink. Lessons were then continued until 12.00 am when we had to get ready for our midday meal.

One of my pet hates was spinach, which was served every lunchtime because Mother Superior thought it good for you, and the convent grew two fields of the stuff! (Unfortunately for us children.)

We sat at a long refrectory table for our meals, which had a long ledge under it, and as far as my hand could reach there were 'lumps of spinach'. As I was never hauled over the coals for it, I could only surmise that the worker nuns kept their own council; or no one ever dusted that ledge!

After lunch we had a two hour compulsory siesta before forming up into a crocodile — in pairs, with a nun at the head of the column, two nuns each side and another bringing up the rear — on no account were we allowed to talk to each other on our long walk down to the sea front. We were allowed a little latitude then and could speak quietly to each other whilst walking up and down the promenade, until it was time to return for tea. How we tried to get out of that tedious walk, pleading headaches, sickness and any other thing we could think of, but all our pleas and excuses fell on deaf ears. All that sea, and I couldn't go swimming!

Tea over, we would go into the so-called leisure room, where we had to walk about for half an hour with books on our heads in order to give us poise; hopefully as graceful a walk as the Zulu women had. We could then sit and talk or read for the next hour, until it was time for our baths. I never did get used to having a ten minute bath — and with my shift on! It was considered sinful to look at one's body! You always had a senior girl sitting in the bathroom to make sure you behaved yourself and didn't go over the allotted time.

As far as lessons were concerned I was average except for sewing, in which I never made the grade. The unhemmed part of the handkerchief I was making never seemed to get any shorter, as my stitches were never small enough, and I was forever having to take them out again. I found it very difficult to hold the needle correctly so that the stitch either went to the left or right but never centre. I was never able to give that handkerchief away as a present as it was far too dirty!

Arithmetic, though, was my favourite and best subject, and I was always in the top grade. For this I must thank my first teacher, the tutor of my brothers, as he had made it so interesting either by using sweets or fruit. He would add, subtract, multiply and even use them for fractions by halving, quartering, etc; at the end of the lesson whoever had achieved the highest marks won them all as a prize. No wonder I always remembered my figures and tables.

The only time we were allowed to laugh or giggle was when a funny story was being read aloud to us in leisure time, otherwise we were always being told 'God loves silence'. We were always very careful to obey that golden rule, otherwise the nuns made sure that no one spoke to you for the next couple of hours. Close friendships were also discouraged amongst the girls, but somehow we always seemed to manage to manoeuvre ourselves next to the person we liked best!

Altogether I was at the convent about eighteen months, during holiday times as well. I was amazed, one day, when out on our crocodile walk, that one of our old houseboys, called James, came rushing over and told me that my grandparents were back in Cape Town and would be in Durban in a day or two. Arrangements had been made for him to come and fetch me the next evening, so that I would be at home to greet them. I was so excited that I hardly slept a wink all night and was ready, with my bags packed, long before he arrived.

I thought I was in fairyland when James took me home on the tram that night. There is no such thing as twilight in South Africa, only a dark velvety night, so you can imagine how wonderful Durban looked with all the lights on, from the top of an open tram. To crown my happiness when I arrived home, a bush by the front door was covered in glow-worms. I shall never forget those two beautiful pictures of Durban as long as I live.

What a wonderful feeling it was to be back with my grandparents once more, even though they gave me the sad news of our having to leave South Africa in a couple of weeks — this time for good.

Chapter 17

Travelling home to England on the P & O liner the Barrabool

What a pity all good things have to come to an end. I was truly sorry to say goodbye to South Africa, although I was looking forward to travelling in a passenger liner once more. So, in December 1927 we left Durban in the *Barrabool*, one of the P & O Steam Navigation Company's ships. She had been built to carry about 1,200 passengers, and had been especially built for the expanding post-war migrant traffic, via the Cape. She was made in Belfast by Hartland and Wolff.

As soon as we boarded the ship we were given mugs of Bovril, with hard-tack biscuits, which were supposed to stop you getting seasick.

On Christmas Day we all had a wonderful surprise. Early in the morning we heard a plane overhead, and all the children dressed in a hurry and rushed up on deck. I was one of the first up and was very, very excited. Looking up, I saw a rope-ladder hanging from the plane, and who should be descending it but Father Xmas, with a great big bag of presents on his back! How we all cheered and clapped.

We had to go to the dining room for our breakfast, and by the side of each plate was a small gift. When we finished we attended a carol service which was held round a large Xmas tree, with Father Xmas standing next to it. What a thrill it was to hear Santa call you by name to give you a present.

The whole of the ship had been decorated with holly, mistletoe and streamers, and fairy-lights had been hung all over the top of the decks. It looked wonderful.

Usually we children had an earlier dinner than the adults, and then we had to go to the children's play area to be looked after by a nurse, but today being Xmas, all the grown-ups joined us, wearing funny hats. The men put on false noses with moustaches attached, whilst the women wore very pretty masks. What a noise we all made with our laughing and singing together.

After dinner there was a Punch and Judy show, and games had also been organised. Father Xmas then said goodbye. It was about 4.00 pm, so we all trooped up on the deck to wave to him as he flew away.

In the evening a fancy dress party was held and my brother and I won first prize. Jack went as 'after the cup final' and wore very torn clothes, jersey and shorts. He was covered in mud taken from the potted plants in the saloon, and mixed with soot from the funnel of the liner. He had sticking plaster on his hands, knees and face, and his arm in a sling. Someone had even found a football from somewhere, which he held under his other arm.

I went as 'Miss Powder Puff' and wore a mini fur crinoline, and a silky blue-ribboned Juliette cap with a huge swansdown powder puff on top. I also had a small face mirror, and a swansdown powder puff tied to my wrist by loose ribbons, so that I could hold them when necessary. What a Christmas! One that I'm sure no one could forget.

One of the saddest moments of the journey was the death of an old man, whom I had befriended and who had regaled me with stories of his childhood in the middle 1870s. It was a beautiful morning, calm and serene with a clear blue sky over a sparkling sea, when I watched his funeral taking place. The coffin was covered with a Union Jack and carried by six sailors, who gently placed it on the deck near a slipway, where a plank had been hooked onto one of the lower rails in a gently sloping position just above the sea.

I listened very intently to the funeral service, given by the ship's minister and captain, who then committed his body into the sea, and his soul into God's keeping. It was a most moving sight to see the coffin slowly sliding into the sea, with hardly a ripple, and the flag gradually and gently being trailed off. Wreathes were then placed on the waves at the spot where the coffin had submerged.

At first, in my imagination, I felt as though I was dreaming and watching a scene in a play which had nothing to do with me; suddenly I awoke to the realization that I could have been witnessing my own mother's funeral in 1915, when she was also buried in that deep, silent ocean. For the first time in my short life I really felt the grievous loss of my mother, and learnt the meaning of death! It also brought to mind a poem I'd heard somewhere and which seemed appropriate to a funeral at sea:

> Washed by the changing tide,
> Drifting afar.
> Anchored to no sea bed
> Or the unchartered sky,
> But drifting instead
> Unpiloted.
> The tide impels,
> Sunk in the silent seas
> Drifting afar, scraping the shells.

After my tears I consoled myself with the thought that now my mother would have someone to keep her company!

Next day we were at Las Palmas, where many little rowing boats came alongside the liner, with all kinds of 'goodies' to barter. The passengers would throw silver into the clear sea, just to watch the little boys dive in and catch the money before it disappeared. One of the sailors — nicknamed 'Fine An' because of his habit of saying 'Fine An' when asked what the weather would be like! — bought me a pillow-slip of gifts, but the only one I remember was a small crinolined doll in a highly polished walnut shell, which was kept closed by a large hook and eye.

One day one of the sailors asked Grandfather if my brother and I could go with him to see the refrigeration room. Before we went we had to wrap up well in two pairs of socks, gloves and coats, as the temperature was well below zero.

There were mounds and mounds of butter and ice-cream, and great carcasses of meat; plenty of fresh fruit and vegetables, and many other kinds of food. When we left we were given great 'dollops' of ice-cream for our tea.

I had a very frightening experience, along with the other passengers. It happened just after we had crossed into the Bay of Biscay. One minute the sea looked like a mill-pond, it was so still and glassy, with flying fish skimming the surface. All of a sudden there was a loud report — so loud we thought a bomb had exploded. It seemed that the yard-arm, with plumb-line attached, had snapped in half like a matchstick. It was actually as thick as the trunk of an oak tree, so you can imagine the noise when it broke in half. This was the beginning of three very frightening days and nights of storm. The liner rolled so heavily that it seemed as if she would roll right over, but fortunately she never did. It was quite impossible to walk straight and we lived and slept in our life-jackets. After deck-practice, we were all allocated places, either in the lounge, library or dining room, in order that the crew knew where we were in case of an emergency.

That old sailor 'Fine An' told me that we were extremely lucky to be travelling on the *Barrabool*, as she was one of the steadiest of the P & O liners; and that was why we were still afloat after being tossed about like a matchbox between the waves.

What a lot of laughter there was when we crossed the Equator, as any male passenger who was sailing over it for the first time was stripped, dressed in a swimsuit and thrown into the swimming pool, where King Neptune (God of the Sea) sat on his throne, with his trident in his hand and surrounded by his assistants, who pushed the poor hapless victim under the water. This unfortunate being would then be scrubbed and scrubbed with a scrubbing-brush, and shaved with plenty of lather and a huge razor, until he begged for mercy. No one ever objected and everyone joined in most heartily with the merriment, as the 'victim' enjoyed it as much as the onlookers.

Nearly all the children on board used to get up early and go up on deck wearing their swimsuits — which by the way were one-piece, with quarter-length sleeves, and legs that came half-way down the thigh — as the sailors would be hosing and swabbing the decks. As soon as they saw us they would direct the water our way, giving us a proper drenching! How we loved it.

I have now come to the end of my much travelled childhood and I hope, dear reader, that you enjoyed reading it as much as I did, remembering and writing down my very vivid memories of it.